T0194460

Finding yourself and Accepting the person you Find

Sharon Rampersad

authorHOUSE®

AuthorHouse™
1663 Liberty Drive
Bloomington, IN 47403
www.authorhouse.com
Phone: 1 (800) 839-8640

Published by AuthorHouse 06/11/2020

ISBN: 978-1-7283-6422-3 (sc)
ISBN: 978-1-7283-6421-6 (e)

Library of Congress Control Number: 2020910584

Print information available on the last page.

Contents

Chapter 1

Taking control

When my son's father and I broke up, I made a conscious decision to not have any serious relationships for the better part of his childhood. I had seen too many situations where a woman got involved with a man and her children became secondary to the relationship. This was not a position I wanted to put my son in. I have friends who dated while their children were growing up and met other people. It took a lot of time and sitters and they had emotional ups and downs. There is nothing wrong with this path and it works out well for some people. I didn't want to commit that kind of time and effort to building a new relationship, at that time. For this reason, I have years of casual dating and experiences to share. I have a great time being single. People fascinate me, so any chance I get to learn about human nature appeals to me. I have absorbed more information than I can fit into one book, but we will begin with one.

Right after I got out of my 10 year relationship (but closer to 12), I got into a temporary rebound situation that broke my heart. It's easy to get attached to someone when you're coming out of a relationship. He said and did the right things. He made me feel good and happy. It was a good distraction for me. He helped me see my strength and challenged me to be better, on my own. I learned a lot about myself during that time. My taste had changed entirely, I went the exact opposite direction of what my ex was. It was an agreeable situation for both parties for a time. Then something happened, things changed. I noticed he kept me at arm's length, but I never really understood why until later on, when things ended. Now I appreciate it to be a form of self-preservation. If you don't want to let yourself get close to someone, you allow yourself to assign a particular function in your life to that person. It's easier to walk away when you're ready.

My version of crazy is by no means close to some of the stories I have heard. I just texted and argued. In retrospect, this behavior to me is just as horrifying as showing up at his door after work one day. It was hard to see him daily, I could not avoid that. I know it's difficult to register yourself to be acting like a crazy person when you're doing it. It took me a long time to get over that situation, before I finally got a grip to let it be over. Now I look back on that time and marvel at my passion for someone I feel nothing for today. It took time for me to heal and I couldn't even really be all that upset with him, if I take ownership for my part of that situation. He was always honest with me. There was no future for the relationship, it was what it was. I had let myself get attached and become dependent on him. Dependence doesn't need to be financial. Emotional can be just as crippling, when it is removed. Now, my goal is to preserve my dignity above anything else.

I don't think any relationship is ever a waste of time. There is time I wish I had not wasted, but even in those cases, there is a lesson to be learned. I learned from each one, in some way. I learn about myself daily and how I process information and people. I've also learned a lot about men and how they think, from all aspects. The relationships that I can't associate a lesson to, are at bare minimum an experience that will serve me, at some point in the future. Experiences are meant to be pondered and reviewed, at some point. It always offers information that helps me save time and navigate situations with a bit more clarity each time.

Recently, one of my girlfriends told me about this situation where a man she's seeing is being stalked by a young woman. She's going over to his place to drop things off regularly, months after they broke up. He had to block her on all social media and ask his family to do the same. She even tried to engage her family into her attempts to woo him back. Thankfully I have no concept of behaving in this particular manner. This is a good example of a 'crazy girl'. But in both situations, there is one person trying to create a situation to open the lines of communication while the other is trying to shut the door on them.

I am fortunate that others have often looked at me as someone to talk to. This not only allows me to multiply my experience, but also to share my knowledge. In part, this is where some of the inspiration for writing this book comes from. Experiences are meant to be learned from. What good is this information if I keep it to myself? The people in my life enjoy my perspective on situations and some of the stories I have to share. After speaking with other women over the years, some of the ideas can be of value to everyone.

We get lost in drama, the daily pressures our lives, common sense sometimes takes leave before we realize. Most of what I have to say isn't new or revolutionary, but sometimes a different perspective and a reason to think differently can shed new light on a situation that seemed hopeless, at first.

Hindsight is 20/20. I look back on my situation and try not to be too hard on myself about it. I'm human. I learned a lot to help me through the rest of my life. I have never forgotten anything that impacted my life. There are things I wish I had done differently. But this is where learning happens. The time has passed to fix anything. Sometimes we have to suck it up and admit it's time to move on. I can be confident it won't happen again, let it be. Time will tell. Some women have no problem with 'being a fool for love'….I have a problem with it.

Things I now ask myself are:

- What is this behavior saying about me?
- Am I presenting myself in a manner that is appealing?
- Would I want someone behaving like this?
- Is this behavior reflective of pride and self-respect?
- Am I demonstrating my value and sense of self-worth?

Another key point I ask myself now is what do I like about this person? Have they done anything for me to like them? These are important questions that I have to ask myself because I am too trusting. I take people at their word. I don't lie, I have no reason to, and therefore I assume other people are the same. This is my mistake. People need to earn trust, it shouldn't be given freely. I need to ask better questions before making decisions about people. There is nothing wrong with giving other people a chance, giving someone an opportunity to get to know me doesn't mean I should trust them too quickly, either. If someone wants to make an impression on you, they will. If they want you to like them, they will offer you a reason to do so. Liking people for who they are is what I call my friends, not my partner.

Hearing about my friends' situations and comparing them to my own, I notice there are a few key points all of our situations have in common:

If a man wants you, he will let you know. He will figure it out. And rejection is something they expect. It will NOT deter him. You don't need to chase.

> *I can recount numerous situations where I told a guy 'no'. No mixed signals, no games. And if anything, these were the men that pursued me more. I know what it's like to be wanted and desired…why am I chasing? Relating back to my other experiences with romance, the men that loved me best and longest were the ones that did the pursuing. Chasing anybody makes me look desperate, which nobody finds attractive. Thinking of the previous times I learned this puts my mind back on the right track.*

If he doesn't want to be with you, he will make that painfully clear through his actions and behavior.

Many of us have been in situations where things changed. I can recall a situation where my rebound relationship ended and I tried to hang on to him well past the expiry date. What results did this yield? Some could make it sound sweet and romantic. I call it crazy and desperate, which, as I already mentioned, is not an appealing quality. Looking for reasons to see him, text him, call him. Trying to figure out ways to make him see. I look back on it now and wonder, who was that woman? One of my friends once said to me, 'you can't be hard on yourself for not knowing how to behave in a situation you've never been through before'. The truth is we are all trying to figure things out. Nobody's perfect and we all make mistakes. Not looking honestly at each person's actions in the situation is where we fall short and start doing things they perceive to be 'crazy'.

To put it plainly, if he isn't appreciating you, it's because he doesn't.

If he isn't coming for you, you don't need to remind him that you're there.

Referring back to my time in crazy town, he told me he didn't want to be with me anymore. He showed me he didn't want to be with me anymore. He was seeing other women, living his life. And here I was trying to recapture something that was long dead. I remember being out one night with some of my girlfriends. I looked over at one of them and saw text messages from him. We impose pain on ourselves and then get mad at the other person because they aren't responding the way we want them to.

I cannot control anything in a situation but myself and my behavior. All I could do was let go.

I have learned to appreciate the female friends that I have as a mother much more than I did in my youth. Where they were just people to have fun with earlier in life, they serve so many more functions as an adult. Friends can be wonderful consultants. They are a fabulous support system, in varying degrees, and if selected wisely. They can be a fountain of entertainment. I prefer to be a listener than a talker. When I have personal issues of my own, it's good to ask others about themselves and focus on what they have to say than to think about my own problem. Often, a solution comes when my mind is clear, after some time has passed. My temper is less inflamed and I have had time to analyze the situation from a more rational and less emotional perspective. Speaking and making decisions fueled by emotions often brought me more problems to solve than solutions.

When I was younger, arguments, disagreements, and fights with my partner would disrupt my life to no end. It would consume my thoughts and drive me crazy because of the lack of resolution. There are times when you can't sleep, you can't eat, and you can't focus. One day I started evaluating some of my male friends. Listening to their stories about getting into an argument with their girlfriend and going out and having a great time without her, as a result of the disagreement. Maybe they were bothered, but you couldn't tell because they were out enjoying their life. Each would deal with his relationship when he was done having his fun. This made me start to think, maybe there is some sense is what once appeared to be a selfish act. Where was the fault in taking a step back and giving both parties some time to cool down and reflect? Maybe instead of rejecting this idea as insensitive and thoughtless, I might learn something. I'm not saying I will walk away from a situation every time, but I can be more understanding if someone else does it now. It takes some time, but it comes with practice.

We live in a world where sex and love are not mutually exclusive. It's easier to find someone to love you for a night than to love you for a lifetime. I allowed myself to be swept up in this new attitude from the one I had growing up. It fit with what I wanted at that time. After having had 2 intense relationships already, I was exhausted and gave up on the idea of love for myself. Why want a relationship right away? There is so much unknown territory. It's almost like crawling out of a cave for the first time in 10 years… the light is blinding, there is so much to see. So many different things to look at, all at the same time. That was my first time being single. For me, there was so much I didn't know, so much I was curious about. Only having lived the life that I have can I say I became curious about things I didn't even know I would be curious about. There are many interpretations of dating. It can be a convenient way to satisfy your needs and not have to deal with the inconvenient aspects of the relationship experience. Or it can be the way you find someone to share your life with. I used to think it all depends on the person and what they are looking for at the time. Now I think it depends on the person and how they perceive the person they are talking to.

We all change throughout the course of our lifetime. People don't change….until they have a compelling reason to want to change for themselves. Only considering adulthood, I can count the number of major life changing events, but I can't count how many versions of myself I have had because learning is an ongoing process and I am constantly evolving. I haven't always been in love with every version of myself, but the foundation has never strayed from being anything less than strong and resilient. That foundation is what has sometimes given me the drive that I need to improve the other areas of my life. It takes strength to look at yourself and be honest. It's the hardest thing I have to do on a regular basis. But I saw a YouTube video once that reminded me, nobody owes it to you to invest in your dreams. Nobody owes it to me to help me reach my dreams. That's why they belong to me. This changed the way I see the world and made me think of my childhood. I gave up dreams I had in youth because someone else told me I shouldn't have them. They weren't realistic. I can't blame a child for not knowing better, but I regret not having more passion for the dreams that I had. They have since been replaced, and nothing stops me from starting again, but the time lost is what I mourn for.

So where I stopped asking 'Why do I do these things to myself?', and learned to invest that desire for love into pushing myself to get the things done that I needed to. I look at the person I am at the beginning of this book and the person who evolves throughout the course of the book, it's all about changes that happen.

People change every day through experience and knowledge, as a way of better navigating life. Every waking moment is an opportunity to learn, if we are willing to take the time to see the lessons that are being presented. "People don't change" is reserved for the people who refuse to see and don't want to grow.

Chapter 2

Finding self-esteem

When my relationship ended after 10 years, it was not an easy decision to make. We spent years trying to fix things and deciding what to do. I was scared to be on my own raising a child. I questioned if it was something I could do daily. My desire to be free and have my own space outweighed my fear of the unknown. Once we made the decision to separate, I started preparing for that change, and it was like a weight had been lifted. The anxiety of moving and having to take care of this little person on my own was stressful, if I let myself think about it too much, so I didn't. There are times when it's just easier to focus on the task at hand and getting that accomplished, worry about the stress of getting it all done later. It's easy to say I should have done this sooner. But the truth is, we all do things when we are ready to do them.

Many women wait years to leave unhappy situations. When my friends ask me what made me decide to leave? My initial response was I saw the effects that an unhappy home was having on my son. He was acting up in daycare, fighting with other children. He would be running from one room to another when he was home so he could spend time with both of his parents. After thinking about it, my desire to go our separate ways outweighed my fear of being a single mother and any challenges that might bring. It felt like we were all slowing dying a little bit every day being trapped in a negative situation. I will commit myself to a situation completely, I will give it 110% effort. I stayed longer in that relationship than I would in any situation today, with the benefit of experience behind me. When you have a family, there is always a compelling reason to want to fix things until you get to that point where nothing can be done. Moving forward, if I don't see any reason to stay, I will leave. The only unconditional love I consider valid is a parent's love for their child/children. This is the only time someone ever came into my life that I feel obligated to love and care for.

Every couple gets together because both parties filled a need in the other person. Rarely has anyone ever told me they just fell in love with the other person because they were who they were. There is always some reason for why people end up together. Whether it be attention, affection, material, emotional, intellectual, there is always a reason. More likely, there are multiple reasons. When one person decides to withdraw some or all of the reasons that made their partner fall in love, should they continue to be in love? Particularly the ones that are important to the other person. Relationships begin for a reason. This is why I do not consider them to be based on unconditional love.

We are all an evolving entity, every waking moment is an opportunity to learn something. Every experience, situation and relationship is also contribution to growth. Growing and expanding into the Universe, each in our own special way. This is one of the ways I see the contributions we each make to society. Every experience contributes to the depth of our character and energy we put out into the world.

I did not appreciate other women the way I do now, when I was younger. Like many other women I have met, I didn't like other women in my late teens and early twenties. Only after I became a mother was I able to identify with other women and start trying to understand their situations. Instead of judging, try to put myself in their position. I have no idea what it is to live anyone else's life but my own. Who am I to judge them? It started with other mothers and over time evolved to all women. We are all amazing beings and have so much to offer one another. In youth, primal instincts cause young women to mistrust and dislike one another out of competition. Once I had a child all of those preconceived notions seemed to melt away. I think motherhood probably made me more likeable to other women, as well.

Being a single mother can feel lonely when you don't have friends who are also mothers. I remember when my son was in daycare, most of the friends I had were single. It felt like every time they went out, I had to go pick up my son. Every time I had a sitter or someone to watch my son, everybody had things to do. It can be a frustrating adjustment. One day, when I had left my son with my mom for the night, I wanted to go out. Everyone was busy but I wanted to go dancing and tired of waiting for people to do what I want to do. I told myself 'if you continue waiting for people to do things, you will never get anything done in life.' I forgot about any feelings I might have about going out alone, got dressed and went out. I remember I was wearing black pants and a black shirt that night because a man came over and asked me if I was a bouncer. Being only 5'2" and incapable of throwing anybody anywhere, I started laughing. He said, "Well, you are wearing all black, holding a water bottle." It turned out he and his friends were in Montreal from New York for a bachelor party. I partied and danced with them until I was ready to disappear, and then left. That was a great night I would never have had if I had allowed my fears of doing things on my own to control me.

The great thing about having kids, however, is that when they're young, they're a great way to meet new people. I made numerous friends when my son was younger because he had playdates and made friends on the playground. It's hard, especially after a long day at work, but letting your child run around with their friends after school for 30 minutes can be helpful on multiple levels. Children and school are also instant conversation topics. So while the children run around with their friends is a potential time to meet people you can relate to, if nothing else. After school, most parents welcome conversation of another parent while their child runs around, ignoring them. I know it isn't a simple task for everyone, but creating a network of other parents that you can talk to helps. It was only through talking to some of the other mothers did I realize my son wasn't unique in not listening and acting up in class. He was being a normal little boy. I would never have known this if I hadn't taken the time to let my child play a little bit after school sometimes. You don't have to like everybody, you don't have to talk to everybody. But it can help your child if you are able to show them how to make friends through making friends yourself.

All it takes is one or 2 people to start creating yourself a network of people you could potentially create friendships with along the way.

Self-esteem is a broad topic, there are many factors that affect it. For most women coming out of a relationship, particularly one that was long term, there is some internal work that needs to be done. First and foremost, acknowledge and appreciate the steps you have taken and challenges you faced to get to this point in your life. This is a great point of reference towards rebuilding your self-confidence. For every living person, **our lives are a living testament to what we are each capable of accomplishing.** Athletes and Olympians, celebrities and famous names in history accomplish things that we marvel at. But just because your life isn't documented and celebrated doesn't mean you aren't great and haven't done amazing things, as well. Changing your life is something that not all people have the strength to accomplish. Some people live their whole life in a miserable situation because they are too scared or insecure to take steps towards creating a happier life for themselves and their loved ones.

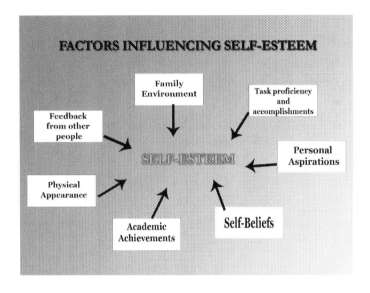

Family Environment: This is not something we have control over. But we do have control over allowing ourselves to believe that we are a product of our environment so there is no hope. There are dozens of famous people that I could name that came from nothing. Some were homeless. Some are now famous celebrities, some millionaires are the unsung hero of their own lives. Looking back on my childhood now, I could criticize and point out the negative things that happened. It wasn't always blissful but I remember that childhood was when I had the most hope for myself and my life. I choose to see everything that happened as events that helped shape me into the person that I am, and I choose what defines me. Not where I came from. Where I came from and how I was or wasn't raised, is an excuse I use to allow myself to stop myself from chasing my dreams.

Task Proficiency and Accomplishments: This is something we also control. Taking pride in your work and abilities is something we might take for granted. Particularly when you are doing a job that doesn't offer any praise or if you are doing something that comes naturally to you. Trying to be the best person I can be and do right by other people. Stand up for what I believe in and what I know to be right. Have integrity in the things that I do and expecting the most of myself, is the least I can hope to accomplish. It isn't always something that can be put in a resume, but little things count. Being able to wake up and get out of bed every day is a blessing because there are people who cannot. To have a job, sometimes any job, is an accomplishment. I've had jobs that I hated, it was sometimes personal torture to force myself to go to these places some days. I might not be particularly proud to have worked at some of the places that I have, but I will always hold my head high because I did what I had to do to get by. I did what I had to until I could create a better situation for myself or a solution was presented. Not an accomplishment for anyone to know but me, but that doesn't make it any less valuable.

Personal Aspirations: We all have dreams and goals. We all live in a world where there isn't enough time to get what needs to get done accomplished. Never mind make time for dreams and personal goals. When my son was younger, I feel like I was always running around. Thinking back, I would be lying if I said I never had time to work on my personal aspirations. I made time to talk to friends for hours at a time. I made time to go out, when I needed to do it. I made time to watch television and movies when I wanted to do that. There is nothing wrong with these activities, but for me to say I never had time to work on myself and my desires, would be a lie. I think I could have

Sharon Rampersad

carved out an hour a week to do something towards my personal aspirations, if I had made it a priority. So, this was something that has always been in my control, but that I had convinced myself I did not have any control over.

Self-Beliefs: This is my favorite part of self-esteem because this is all within our own control. Growing up, I didn't feel the greatest about myself, I was not always taught things that helped my self-esteem. Being a teenager, we start to form beliefs about ourselves and the world. Sometimes these conclusions are harm our self-esteem. Breaking negative thought patterns isn't easy. I can't speak to anyone else's experience in their life, but I can share how I help myself.

One trigger for when my self-beliefs start to spin out of control is when obstacles come up. Financial distress is a relatable area for most. After the initial freak out and panicked thoughts of what am I going to do stage, this might last a few minutes, I pull myself together and start thinking rationally about what my next steps should be. I then remind myself that I do not deal with any loan sharks or other organizations who would kill me for money. Nobody I know is going to die over this. There is a resolution in place. I remind myself that this is not the first time I have owed money to debt collectors. I left a relationship with debt to become a single mother, I worked through that. I have been in debt for thousands of dollars, living at my parents with my child, and no job…I survived that with all limbs intact. The point to my reminding myself of these times is to remind myself that I am stronger that I ever believed I was before I lived through those situations. I can always shock and amazing myself, when I need to. This is what makes me the strong, resilient woman that I am.

Academic Achievement: This is also something we all control, to a degree. I understand that life can get away from you and this becomes less of a priority. I have met women who waited until their children were grown and gone to pursue their dreams. Others struggled and went to school while their children were growing up to make a better life for them all. This depends on the person. Self-development would be able to fall under this category, as well. Not every successful person went to University or even graduated from high school, for that matter. Some people didn't achieve their success until they stopped focusing on traditional education and started chasing their dreams because they believed in their skills and abilities that much. Achievements are things that contribute to your success. Any achievement contributing to your profession, your craft or your personal goals is something you can and should be proud of.

Physical Appearance: This is referring to how you keep and dress the vessel you are in. Do you take care of your hair? Are you well kept? Neat? Do you look and smell clean? When I was a teenager, I was a chubby girl. It's a challenge to dress a bigger body, especially when you're a teenager. I used to watch this show called 'what not to wear' religiously. It was a show catering to everybody because they invited all body types to come on. They would go into someone's home, throw out their whole wardrobe and rebuild them a new one from scratch. They taught you how to dress the body you're in. You don't have to go to a gym or be wealthy to be well dressed and take pride in the body you have. If you aren't happy with the body you have, the only thing that prevents most of us from making the changes we need to make to be happy is ourselves. Many years later, after I had my own child did I get to a point in my life where I needed to start taking care of myself to prove my love for myself.

Feedback from other people: We all love praise and approval. Even those people who don't sometimes like to know they are appreciated. While this is a fact, another fact is also that we really don't need the approval of anyone to do or be what we like. Most advice is offered with good intentions. Especially when it comes from people who love and want the best for you. I do accept the input others have to offer. Most of the time this comes from a good place. Everybody likes to be heard and to know that their suggestions are appreciated. However, wanting to follow your own path is not a bad thing. There are times that I remember doing things for the sake of having the experience.

I will use one of my friends whom I love dearly as an example. There are things that she wants to do in her life, there are experiences she wants to have. However, because she is a good girl and loves her mother, she stops herself. Her thoughts of 'what will my mother think?' stop her from doing the things she wants to do. She knows her mother would be disappointed or not approve. She hears her mother's voice in her head.

We all do. I'm no different than anybody else in hearing my mother's voice trying to guide my decisions in life. The difference, for me, is I realized that my parents lived their own lives. It didn't seem like it, but I was listening when they told me, despite people telling us not to do it, we still followed our dream, anyways.

These are the areas to address when you want to make yourself feel better and stronger. It isn't necessary to work on them all at the same time. But if you want to start feeling better about yourself, work on the areas you have control over and take pride in the accomplishments you make in those directions.

Life is too short to allow yourself to be unhappy or unappreciated, even to yourself.

Chapter 3

Positivity

Positivity is an area that can be difficult to maintain. Being positive is not always easy when you have thoughts constantly running through your mind. I had to take care of this little person and pay all of the bills myself. I had a lot of stress and anxiety. I was starting a new job in a new industry. I started to watch videos on motivation at that new job that changed my life. One video led to another, I started seeing different kinds of motivation from different kinds of people. The things that people are capable of. The kind of person that I want to show up as in the world. I started to read books and articles about self-improvement and success stories. Anything that I could use to keep pushing myself forward. The reality is life is how you perceive it. People have the ability to do amazing things when they have the will to do it, or have no other option. Successful people see negative situations as a positive, and an opportunity to learn and grow.

There are no negative situations, every obstacle I come across in my life really has made me better, especially the painful ones. Comfortable, it isn't a bad thing. Some people want a comfortable life they can maintain, they aren't moving backwards, but forward movement is slow and not a top priority. Slow and steady is perfectly fine for them to finish the race. Discomfort and pain is often the time we experience the most growth. I can't remember a time that I was scared and uncomfortable that I didn't experience growth during or afterwards, or both. More often than not, it was in those times that I was able to show myself that I am capable of much more than I give myself credit.

Maybe you don't see the cup as half full. There are people who see the world from a place of loss rather than a place of abundance. Maybe it might be easier for you to view situations as neither good nor bad. They are merely obstacles you need to overcome to help make you better. Just things you live through that help you down the road. No bad time in my life has ever lasted forever, it was more about seeing the good parts of life, and getting through those bad parts until that time passed. A lot of the things that I have experienced, have helped me avoid the some of the same pains moving forward but the most rewarding use I get out of them is sharing them with others.

When I was growing up, I was taught to keep to myself. Keep information to myself. Don't share too much about myself with others. I have learned that there is some merit to this attitude. I've met many people throughout the course of my life who thought this way, if they said it or not. If you come across enough disappointing people, it can cause someone to stop wanting to share. I've experienced this feeling myself. But I have a loving heart. More importantly, however, is that this thinking goes against everything I learned about becoming successful and growing into the Universe. So I taught myself to start thinking differently.

I had a friend I knew for years. She was there before my son was born up until the time my son's father and I broke up. After all we had been through, after all we had shared, I thought she would have been my friend forever, but she decided he would take guardianship of her when we broke up. When you put your trust in someone and end up disappointed, it makes it hard to trust someone again. So to apply this principal to people works, as well. Most people, in general, are both good and bad. She was a good friend for the time that we were friends. I learned from her. We shared our life experiences. I have learned to appreciate, every time a friend has walked out of my life, that I had the opportunity share some of their experiences. Something coming to an end doesn't diminish the experiences you shared. When friendships end, there is little reason to hold on to any resentment or hate. It was a learning experience, more likely multiple experiences. I didn't let it stop me from making new friends in my life and moving on.

Challenging relationships with challenging people are to prepare me for later things in life. I taught sales as a vocation for a session, not too long ago. When I was teaching, I had one particular student. He showed up late. Would be on his phone when he did show up. Treated me dismissively, but would still show up to class, sit at the front, and ignore me. I did my best to work with him in a pleasant way. I would mention his tardiness with a touch of humor when he would show up in the middle of class. I offered assistance and still tried to include him in class discussions. The only time, however, that he actually felt my pain was when he found a job teaching himself during my course. He came after his first week teaching and sympathized with me for putting up with his behavior.

I've observed this many times in my life, with people much closer to me in some cases, who judged a situation based on nothing more than their opinions. We don't always know where someone is coming from when we make decisions about them. Not everybody has the empathy to think beyond their own understanding of a situation. It's easy to assume what motherhood is like and how you would be in that situation, if you have never been a mother and don't know the demands. One of my relatives didn't understand how it could be so difficult for me to be a single mother until she and her husband had a child of their own to raise together. She was able to identify with the idea of needing time for yourself, when raising a child. Only then, was she able to understand my position with empathy. Most people have an opinion instead of a helping hand.

In both situation everybody had a lesson to learn about empathy. My task was to identify and remember that some people are unable to put themselves in someone else's shoes. Some people will never understand another point of view until they are put in the same position. It isn't their fault, they are just not able to think outside of their own experience. I didn't spend too much time dwelling on these situations. In time they were presented an opportunity to feel their own interpretations of what it's like to be in someone else's position. They came to a better understanding because they had to experience it firsthand.

Being positive isn't a course you take, there is plenty of research you can do and books you can read, but here are some of the steps that I use to help me maintain my positive attitude towards life:

1. Being positive is a choice. It is easy to let yourself go to a negative place when bad things happen. 'Why me?' is a favorite among many. I used to feel the same way. This does not help solve anything. Now when bad things happen, I get a hold of myself. I truly believe now that **every outcome is in my best interest**. I might not always see how or why in that moment, but this is always my guiding light in every situation.

2. Rid yourself of negativity. Negativity really does breed negativity. I think back on some of the conversations I had when I was younger. Some of the ladies' nights I went to with my girlfriends. One friend would start complaining about her man and next thing you know all 6 women are talking about their partner's flaws. I'm not saying to get rid of your friends, but try talking about other things, or choose more closely how you spend time in groups. **Focus on positive relationships, have conversations to help build and improve your life.**

3. If you don't see the positive in a situation, look for it. I don't remember one time I could not see the positive in any situation that I was presented with. **The bare minimum that I can draw from any challenge is that it was a learning experience**. Often, there is much more to it than that, but in some cases time needs to pass for this to become obvious, if it becomes obvious at all.

4. Reinforce positivity in yourself. This is the 'easiest' way you can start reinforcing a more positive outlook on life. Tell yourself you "I look good!" We all have things about ourselves we love and appreciate. **We all have our own special gifts that make us unique and special in our own way. We should all acknowledge and appreciate these gifts.**

5. Share positivity with others. People want to be reassured that 'everything is going to be ok' and 'it's not as bad as you think'. This can be in a variety of ways. You don't have to solve anyone's problems. You would be surprised how much a genuine smile or compliment can make all the difference in someone's day. Just to know you have a shoulder to cry on can give someone the support they need to keep going. **Tell the people you love that you love them and how much they mean to you.**

At one point in my life, I had a son in junior high, I had to move back in with my parents and I owed close to 10K in debt that I had to clear up before I could do anything. No money. No job. It was one of the most miserable times of my life. Depressing and the situation seemed hopeless. I have had a few times in life where I wanted to give up. Fighting to move forward and stay strong isn't always easy. There were times that I wanted to stop trying altogether. There are times that you feel like nothing is happening… there is no light at the end of the tunnel. But like everything in life, nothing happens overnight. Particularly the things that mean something. Sometimes the best thing is to take things one day at a time. If for nothing more than to help you find the motivation to get out of bed every day.

The thing that drives me most to find that motivation is my fear that if I allowed myself to get into a hopeless state of mind, I won't be able to bring myself out of it. I probably could have stayed living at my parents' for much longer than the 16 months that it took for me to get back on my feet. When you have someone depending on you, giving up is not a conceivable option. I'm too concerned with being a good role model and demonstrating the ability to find success in adversity. I have someone watching how I respond to the world and things that happen to me in it much more carefully that I think. I'm thankful that my parents didn't let me get too comfortable. It was anxiety every time I had to go home. I felt like my failures were staring me in the face every time I looked at my family.

I focused more on taking better care of my health and made a routine of going to the gym first thing in the morning. After that, I would spend a couple of hours every morning to looking for a job. The rest of my days were spent taking courses, learning and doing things to improve myself and my abilities. In this particular instance, within 6 months, I ended up finding a great job that helped me get my life in order and find a new apartment. It was a starting point. At that point, the motivator was to get myself out of this situation I had created. It took me another 9 months to be in a position to look for and get an apartment.

No bad situation lasts forever if you keep working towards a solution. Even if it appears to be hopeless. I use this thought, paired with my past experiences to help pull me through. Looking back, things could have been much worse. I am grateful that my parents opened their home to me in my time of need. I am fortunate that my son was accepting of the situation and did not contribute to my anxiety. I was able to keep my car so I could still get around. Looking back now, I'm happy my parents made me uncomfortable. They gave me the push I needed to get back on my feet. When you're living in it, you can't always see the benefits. But that doesn't mean they aren't there.

I had a guy I have been friends with for the last few years who went through a similar situation, having to give up his apartment and move back in with his parents. We are about the same age, only difference being he has no children. Three years and counting, he is still 'getting his life together', living with his parents. From the discussions we've had, his parents were more welcoming and happy to have him back home. They go on vacation, he has the place to himself sometimes. Perhaps if my parents had made me feel more welcome and free to occupy space, I might still be living with them instead of supporting myself and my son myself in our own home.

Support isn't always warm and fuzzy. Sometimes the things we say to someone out of love can seem harsh and cruel, at first. Sometimes hard and direct is the only way to get the message across in an effective way. I think about myself, I may not always appreciate it in the moment, but tough has helped me find the motivation I needed to keep pushing myself forward. If my parents had been patting me on the back and reassuring me everything would be ok, it wouldn't have helped me achieve anything. It might have made me feel better in that moment, but that makes very little contribution to me getting out of the position I had created for myself. I needed discomfort to remind me that I need my own space in the world. During that time, all I could keep saying to myself is I need to get my life together and this can never happen again. The reminder that I am strong and independent every day helped me change my situation faster than I think I would have otherwise.

I have had times when I was broke, no money to buy a carton of milk, no idea how we would eat that week, and then by some miracle, a check would show up in my mail box from my former employer for bonuses not yet paid. Or I would get a direct deposit of money from the government. I even remember finding a $50 bill in my wallet, as if it appeared out of thin air. I believe **the Universe always takes care of me, as long as I'm a good person with a loving heart.** I have noticed throughout the course of my life this has always been true. This doesn't mean that everything is always roses and sunshine. Quite the opposite. The times that I was broke and that money didn't show up, I always had enough to manage until money did find me. In these cases, I would tell myself wants and needs are not the same thing. Just because I want something does not mean I will have it. Whereas when I need something, it often finds me when I need it the most. It is easier to let yourself be negative than to try to see the positive side of the situation as a reflex. But I assure you, it is always there.

Sometimes it takes someone else pointing out your good fortune before you can see it. When someone tells me their life is going horribly, I try to help find something in their life that is right, to pull their mind away from fixating on the wrong things. There are so many areas of life we can draw on when one part is going badly. For instance, every time a job did not work out. My initial reaction might be to cry or be sad. But that does not mean that my life has now gone down the drain. The first time it happened was devastating. But the thing with experience is the more you collect, the better you become at dealing with situations. I used to hate doing job interviews. So I used every opportunity I could as a chance to improve a different aspect of myself. Improve my resume. Then I improved my cover letter writing skills. I worked in my interview techniques. Worked on things that I should be saying. Improved my knowledge however I could to increase my possibilities of getting the jobs that I wanted.

Motivation is what gets you started, habit is what keeps you on course. One of the things that I have become adamant about in the last few years is working on is my physical fitness. It is a practice in both habit and self-discipline. I understand from experience and comparing myself now to my former selves, I will not have a strong mind without a strong body. They are linked to one another. Exercise helps the mind function more efficiently and deal with stress better, both physically and mentally. I have friends who hate working out. I used to be this way, also. If you keep at it and don't see results, it can be frustrating. Sometimes it's better to get help to get you started. I did. I feel a great sense of pride from taking care of my health more consciously, this helps improve self-esteem, as well. I acknowledge and am very proud of how far I have come and the improvements that I have made. Like most things in life, nothing happens overnight, so this is something I now consciously devote a little bit of time to daily because it is the least I can do for myself.

Single mothers tend to think of themselves last, their

needs come after everyone else's, if there is even any time to address them. I understand this. But taking 30 minutes out of the day, 3 times a week, to commit to doing something for body and mind, is essential. Having built this habit into my life makes me a happier person. A happier me is a better mother to my child and a better person for the world, in general.

Chapter 4

Meeting people

Having been in a relationship in my early twenties, dating didn't actually begin until my early thirties. I don't have much of a gauge as to what it was before adulthood, as I never dated in my teens. I know that I stepped into a foreign world. Fortunately, I learn to adapt quickly and am open to new ideas. For this reason I allowed myself to be open to different ideas and kinds of people. There is no harm in talking and getting to know people. There is information in most people, if you take the time to pay attention. Coming from a place where I was not interested in forming any deep connections, I was able to meet many people on more superficial levels and observe behaviors and how they moved through the world.

The word relationship encompasses the many ranges of associations we have with others. Business relationships, friendships, relationships with family members, acquaintances and peers. We are taught that a soul mate is a romantic partner to live out the rest of your days with. The world has evolved, why shouldn't that belief, as well?

Everyone wants someone to grow old with. In the absence of finding that one true love, what does someone do? Instead of looking at the lack in life, see the abundance. How I see my life is I have my best friend who I have been through many trials with, but we always stay strong and support each other. Minus the physical aspects of a marriage, I have a partner. I have my son, who has, in his teenage years, become someone I can talk to about anything. I have my family, who may not be there every day, but they are always there when I need them. I also have my friends. We all have different lives, but we make time when we can. Not everybody is a shoulder to cry on, but everybody has their value and purpose. Instead of focusing on the one area, there is still considerable abundance to focus on <u>instead.</u>

For some time, my networking pool was my work place. Some people prefer to nothing about work once they have left the building. This is a personal choice. But when you are a single mother and have little opportunity to socialize, one of the best places to meet people. In actuality, a large majority of relationships start in the workplace. You can rest assured they have a job. It can give you an idea of what kind of work ethic and the kinds of values they have. You might be able to spend time with them on lunch hour and breaks. Sometimes these blossom into after work outings and hanging out. Other times they remain professional relationships maintained and cultivated at work. Both are helpful ways of meeting people and creating a network.

Classes and other kinds of activities. Before I became a single mother, I may have been a bit shy to do things like attend a class, movie or any other public function alone. This is no longer the case. It is sometimes difficult to coordinate your schedule to attend a class. To then have to reconsider going because my friend can't make that one with me makes no sense to me anymore. If I spend my life waiting on other people to get everything done that I want to do, I won't get half the things I want to do accomplished. There are people at the class. You have something in common with everyone there because you all just did a class. I know I don't always seem friendly, but 95% of the time, when someone approaches me with a question, I will respond pleasantly. Conversations start with a smile. It takes practice, like anything, to get over the initial awkwardness, but these are people you will see regularly. I've had numerous occasions, in classes, on the street, where just smiling at someone gave them the confidence to approach me.

The gym and other athletic clubs. Another place with like-minded people. Not everybody is in the mood or mindset to make friends when they are working out. But I do know people who play soccer, hockey and basketball on teams where they are able to make friendships with people who they have a common interest with outside of their profession or place or business.

Another way would be through gaming. I have been playing an online interactive video game on my phone for over 3 years now. It was never a place I thought I would have made friends that I talk to on the phone. Some of them don't play the game anymore, but we maintain a friendship, regardless. You don't always need to see people to be friends with them. Some of the best friends I've had in my adult life were people that I didn't get the opportunity to see and speak with regularly, we were just too busy. But every time we have a chance to catch up, it's as if no time has passed at all. My online gaming world falls into this category. It also inadvertently helped improve my communication skills, in yet another way.

I find the general consensus among many women coming out of relationships is that they want new experiences. Something different that the situation they were coming from.

This point brings us to an area of discussion completely unto itself.

Online dating

So after I exhausted my available pools, I started looking for ways to find new people to meet. People outside of my regular circles that I would never meet otherwise. I learned quickly that monogamy appears to be a concept of the past. It seemed like nobody was looking for any kind of long term or lasting relationship. I allowed other people to set the terms. I wanted company and to meet new people. I wasn't looking for anything long term, so I could be more flexible. It really is amazing the kinds of people you can meet online. I have met some truly wonderful people that I maintain friendships with today. Others were a lesson learned. The personalities people portray online entertained me. I have an open mind and love to learn, so for a long time, people I met online were like a puzzle to solve.

"Friends" with benefits doesn't really have anything to do with friendship. That's just a nice way of saying 'I just want to see you when I need to hook up, so don't get too intense'. Very few people actually mean to have a friendship with the other person. That would, after all, make it a relationship, if you did that.

The thing that amazes me the most about online dating,

is just how much people can change behind the anonymity of the internet. All of a sudden, a man you know absolutely would never walk up to you in a bar to ask you your bra size is bold enough to ask for a picture of them. A woman who would be shy in a public setting, might be more willing to share provocative pictures with a stranger. To a degree, you do set the tone for the way people approach you. But there is also that particularly 'special' part of the population that is going to take their shot, anyways, because what do they have to lose but a missed opportunity? For the most part, however, if you allow someone to set the tone for the relationship you're going to have, that is the kind of relationship you're going to get.

It took me a while to compile enough information to notice trends and be able to make some educated assumptions on what was going on in some of these situations. Instead of turning it inward and blaming myself, questioning myself about what is wrong with me. Most of the time, the fault was not mine to own.

In particular I was able to find ways to identify unavailable men quicker when they decided the needs to know did not include their relationship status.

Some of the signs you can look for:

1. 99% of the time, a single man is going to give you his phone number when he wants to take your conversation offline. Almost all of them say they're single. Less available men offer any other app not the phone number they are assigned when they

get their cell phone. That one is restricted to their girlfriend/wife.

2. For the most part, there are specific times of the day that you will hear from a married man. In my experience, it is usually during their work or 'office' hours. Maybe sometimes before work. Maybe on his way home from work. But there isn't much after hours contact. Somehow the man's day gets busier when he gets home.

3. Talking on the phone is not a favorite past time for men who are unavailable, and they prefer not get you too used to activities they cannot maintain. When I think about it, most of the men I've met online don't like talking on the phone, at all. I'm not saying they were all married, merely pointing out that this is something I settled for because I allowed someone else to set the terms.

4. Meetings are sporadic and there are usually time constraints. You aren't a main course, you're a side dish, and people don't spend too much time on the side dish. If he isn't married, and for some reason can never find time to see you, there is something to question. Most of the time single men are available. If they are interested, they will make time for you. If you know for certain he's single and he still doesn't have time for you, then he just isn't that interested. Save yourself some time and cut that loose.

5. They have 'roommates'. It makes me laugh now when I meet a man in his thirties, and older, who tells me he has roommates. At first, I would take this to be a valid excuse. But then I really started

thinking about it. If you have a good job. Drive your own car. If you're dating and know you want to get laid, it makes no sense to me that 90% of the men I meet online have roommates. Considering all of the single male friends I have, they all live on their own. But, it is possible that they have a roommate, if they say they do. However, this makes me to question myself...do I really want to date someone who cannot support himself on his own? It's like these men used this excuse when they were younger and think it's an acceptable excuse now. We need to stop accepting weak excuses and mask it as understanding.

6. Unavailable men assume they are invited or invite themselves to your place. No single man I have ever met has ever tried to invite himself to my place to meet. They have nothing to hide, so they aren't worried about going out in public, they don't worry about where you meet. They don't suggest that they can come over once your child has gone to bed. These are flashing neon lights that this is an unavailable man.

These observations don't always mean someone is a cheater, but they do support the idea that you might want to take a deeper look at their behavior (and perhaps social media). I disqualify anyone who checks too many of these points. I won't do too much digging into social media. I don't care enough to see if I'm right. Behaviors are much more telling and hold more weight than words. I will put an asterisk on social media because this is a very tempting and easy way to buy yourself a one way ticket to crazy town. Merely the knowledge of having seen it might open up the need to lash out and say something, at some point. There is too much temptation. It only inspires negative emotions like jealousy, frustration and anger. Not a good look. I avoid looking bad by avoiding these platforms as much as possible. I don't monitor social media all that closely, I couldn't be bothered. I don't think it's necessary for me to look into these platforms too carefully because action, or lack of it, is enough indication for me now. Taking all of these factors and having seen some of the torture people go through monitoring their ex's social media feeds, I would prefer to preserve my dignity and not open up the possibility of looking like a crazy person.

Some women don't care and can even go as far as to say dating married men is more convenient as a single mother. They are not able to demand much, if any, of your attention. Most of the time you spend together, is pleasant and happy. There is little reason to believe he is every going to lose his mind and become a stalker, he has a wife to worry about maintaining the image of a loyal husband for. If he doesn't care about his wife's feelings, how is this someone else's responsibility? I understand when a woman's husband cheats on her, somehow the other woman is often assigned the blame. We want somewhere to put our rage. As if the man wasn't aware he shouldn't be pursuing other women. I don't think whether or not the other woman was aware of the wife is even relevant. It shouldn't 'slip your mind' that you'll be crawling into bed with your partner at night. Truthfully, if a man is pursuing other women, some evaluation should be done closer to home.

I've encountered married men who are honest about their situations, and other who have lied. The honest ones claimed to be unhappy at home but 'stuck because of the kids'. Others were happy at home, just 'need something different'. Either way, they offer reasons that seem plausible and make them sympathetic creatures. The ones who lied, presented themselves as single. I think either way, if a man wants to cheat on his wife, this is his decision to make and own.

Chapter 5

Setting Goals

A way to support this is to visualize the goals that you have on paper. What would you like to accomplish? Goals have been proven to help people not only meet their goals, but they can also accelerate the time it takes to reach them. Writing them down is a great way to present them to the Universe and to make them a reality of something that you want. In a way, it's making a commitment.

I have never been a fan of the To-do list, however, there is some merit to writing down your goals. In a manner of speaking, it brings them to reality. Setting goals is a great way to help you track progress and to stay the course towards the goals you want to achieve.

Particularly when you approach and execute them in the following way:

There are 3 kinds of goals.

Outcome goals are the end result we are looking for, such as I will lose 30 lbs.

Performance goals are the standards of execution and results achieved towards the outcome goal. They work best when used in conjunction with process goals. Meeting your performance goals on your process goals helps you achieve outcome goals.

If I perform 30 minutes of cardio per day and restrict my caloric intake to 1800 calories daily and drink 2.5 liters of water daily for one month I will lose 10 lbs.

Process/behavioral goals are the activities and actions we take in order to help us achieve the outcome goal.

For example:

- I will do 30 minutes of Cardio per day
- Monitor my caloric intake for everything I eat
- Drink 2-3 liters of water per day
- Eliminate snacking or choose healthier options for one month
- Stop eating food after 7PM

These are meant to be specific, measurable, attainable, relevant and timed. To provide progress and motivation.

Writing goals down makes them more real, they become something tangible. Once they are written down, I can visualize more clearly what actions I can take to move me in that direction. I have never been good at keeping lists, but this is one I practice regularly because I have seen the benefits it has brought to my life since I began.

It's good to have a goal, for nothing other than to give you something to strive for. Having a competitive personality, I embrace this thinking. I compete with everyone for everything I try to accomplish, most of all, with myself. Not everybody is of this mindset. I also have a little rewards system in place where I allow myself to have something after my workout, as a reward for going to the gym. Not something that is going to undo all of my efforts, but something that makes me feel good. But when your goal is a passion, the work you put into it doesn't feel like work. I didn't understand goals until I started building them around the things that I care about. After that, finding the extra push I needed to get me there wasn't as hard to find, anymore.

Sometimes, when times seem at their worst, the best thing to do is put your head down and go until you start to see a light at the end of the tunnel. There are times you just need to believe your hard work is going to pay off in the end. Breaking them down into smaller, attainable goals helps show some progress. Once you start seeing those smaller goals disappearing, you start to feel some kind of forward movement, which builds encouragement to work on other goals that are all contributing to the larger goals which are dreams.

My primary motivators haven't changed drastically over the last few years. These are the things that always push me to get out of bed every day, even on the days when I think I can't do it. It is good to have at least 3, but ideally you want to identify 5. They offer the compelling reasons to start creating the right habits in your life, and to maintain them.

1. My child.

I am a role model, whether I want to be one or not. I have noticed throughout his lifetime, my son subconsciously followed all of my behaviors growing up. And consciously ignored many of the directions and instructions that I offered. What I do, how I behave and how I see life directly impacts my child›s view of the world. Whether I like it or not, I am modeling behavior for another person that he is going to take into the world. If children become accustomed to seeing ambition, passion, and drive, they might not mimic the behavior immediately. But once they find the things they are passionate about, these qualities will come out on their own. As mothers, we are showing our daughters the kinds of women they want to become and showing our sons the kind of women they want to be with.

2. I have a lifestyle I intend to maintain. I like being able to buy what I want and do what I please. This cannot be done on social assistance. My life should only improve. The regressions my life has taken in the past emphasizes this goal for me.

3. Other people have come from less and done so much with their lives. There is nothing that separates me from them but my own desires to succeed. If somebody else can do it, I can too. When I am inactive, I feel guilty because I know I am meant to be doing more and I know I am wasting time that I will never get back.

4. I like making money. My desire to make money and have the things that I want outweighs my desire to sleep in. Pair this with liking to win makes for a very compelling reason for me to need to get out of bed. There is plenty of time to sleep when you are dead. Life is too short to spend too much of it sleeping.

5. I have goals that I need to achieve. I know that the Universe is always pointing me back in this direction, to try to share myself and my experiences with others. Having been in sales all of my adult life, I have studied communication extensively, from numerous aspects. Human relationships

are fascinating. This comes down to following my life path according to my belief system and the direction I see my life being guided.

If you're not happy with something do something to change it or accept it. Things you have no control over, accept and move on. To dwell on it does nothing more than to give you wrinkles and give you gray hair. These are the things I tell myself, often, when I feel like I might want to complain about something in my life. Nobody is going to change it for you. I wasn't happy with myself years ago, so little by little, I worked on the things I wanted to change. Attitude. Perspective on life. My physical appearance. What I have control to change, I will always opt to change before accepting it as my reality.

Chapter 6

Self-Love

One of the things my friends have remarked about me is my confidence. I thought I might share some of the things that I draw on. A big part of my confidence comes from the situations that I have lived through. I don't dwell on my past, but I can't stress enough times how important it is to use those experiences in the future. If I have financial issues, knowing that I have been able to collect large sums of money in the past helps me reassure myself, I will be ok. I can't remember the last time I had a shoulder to cry on about anything. I know I'm not the only person who sometimes longs for a comforting embrace and to be told everything is going to be ok. When it's something you don't have, you learn to do without it. When I stopped longing for this and started thinking about the times I took care of my business in absence of another person's comfort, I started to comfort myself.

We all have bad experiences. We all have memories that haunt us. Embarrassment over ridiculous behavior. Tolerating stupidity from others. Doing stupid things ourselves. There are many memories that I hadn't thought of before starting to write this book. Something I started doing years ago was letting go of the bad experiences. Experiences are something that can paralyze you, when they aren't meant to. They are events that we hang on to for the sake of not moving forward. A negative experience is the perfect reason to give up before you even try. You've already set the expectation for yourself. But if you look at it from a different angle, negative experiences are reasons to see strength that might be unseen forever, without having found a reason to be used.

I tend to forget negative situations or experiences that didn't interest me. Boring people, bad dates, bad movies and events, somehow, they all get flushed out of my memory bank regularly. Sometimes we have particularly bad moments in our life that we fixate on because of the extreme emotion involved in it. The impact it made on our lives. The human mind is amazing, there are times when the mere thought can transport you back to a time, to relive emotions and anxieties from that one experience all over again. Sometimes there are environmental triggers that can't be helped. I still go places that remind me of somebody. But we choose our memories, for the most part.

There is no need to hold on to bad memories, like a security blanket. I think about some of my past heart breaks. Some of them were a safe place to go when I was ready to throw a little pity party and feel sorry for myself. Then I started thinking about their value to my bigger picture. There is always a degree of fear when you are shedding something comfortable. Now I am confident in forgetting these experiences because I realized, I learned the lesson I was supposed to. Experiences are neither good nor bad, it all comes down to individual perception. When you look at it objectively, every experience we are offered is an opportunity to grow and become better. As long as some useful, valuable lesson was learned, there is no reason to hold on to those bad memories. I think we hold on to the negative things we go through in life because we don't understand why they happened. If we don't hold on to it, it might happen again. I feel better about those situations when I look at them as a chance to learn and let go of experiences beyond the lessons they bring…because I don't need them. Just like memories of a bad movie, they get purged from my thoughts.

All changes start with changing the way you think. Processing information, coming to terms, dealing with the past…these are all misconceptions when it comes to moving on with your life. I'm not saying there isn't value is figuring things out, but that can take years, for some people. So what do you do between the time you start and the time you're 'fixed'? My mind understands that things have happened to me in the past, but it also doesn't let me use it as an excuse to stop me from moving forward. Or a reason to beat myself up. Neither of which is useful or helpful to me.

All of our brains are like computers. We all absorb data and calculate results, draw conclusions and find solutions based on the data that is input. I've trained my mind to process information, extract the important data from the experience, which is the lesson. And forget about the rest of it. If something gives me pain, but I got the point of why it happened, how does it serve me to keep reliving that experience? I think many of us love our misery because in a way, it's comforting. It's something to hold on to, instead of looking at yourself honestly. It's an excuse to keep punishing someone for something they did to hurt you. None of which will contribute to learning or improving.

It takes a lot of determination and strength to live a life. It takes even more when you take chances without any knowledge of the outcome. Sometimes it works out, other times you learned some new information. The point is not to dwell on mistakes. I use these memories to remind me that I have been through worse. There is always a solution, I am always able to find one. I just need to keep my composure and start looking at the situation objectively. Thinking about these points, along with whatever others I collect along the way, puts the brakes on me losing my resolve and becoming an emotional basket case.

Up until recently, even when I thought I loved myself, I was wrong. I convinced myself that doing what I want is my way of loving myself. Which, to a degree, is true. There is nothing wrong with living my life as I please. I was living the life I wanted and had no issues with it.

But with age comes wisdom and with wisdom comes enlightenment. Enlightenment is a beautiful word. But feeling it, sometimes, is like a hard kick in the face. It isn't easy to see your flaws or the things you were doing wrong. That, in itself, is an accomplishment because nobody wants to see their faults. But I am never anything short of grateful for the new understanding of life and how to better move in the world because even though I was doing it wrong before, I know now. The past doesn't matter, it won't be coming back. What matters is what I do, from this moment forward, always. So with the epiphany:

You can't really love yourself until you understand and accept the value that you bring to another person.

Came the realization that I haven't been loving myself in a way that demonstrates my value to me or anybody else. I consider the support and help I have offered friends throughout my lifetime, I think of the relationship I had with my son's father and how much I contributed. This then brings me to the question, why do I accept less?

I believe in doing things from the heart. If I want to help someone, I will do it willingly, because I know that Karma will bring my good deeds back to me. I've always felt this way and moved through life with these values in mind. This kind of person can be taken advantage of, especially when it is also a person who doesn't ask for anything in return for kind deeds. I don't do things with ulterior motives, but I started to question who I've done anything for who actually showed some form of appreciation for it. Did that other person show any value for my presence in their life after that, or was I just a convenient pair of hands?

Self-love happens in many ways. For me, it happens in stages, and what helps me to love myself more might not be what someone else needs. Taking note of the things I criticize myself about most is where I started.

For a long time I really didn't like the person I was. I hated what I saw every time I looked in the mirror. I didn't feel good about myself. Every time something goes wrong in my life, my default setting is to work out more, take better care of myself. In my defense, growing up, the reactive behavior was to eat. So there is some progress. My best friend tells me "it's unhealthy" to be so obsessive. My response to that is "I am my favorite obsession." I use my weakness to help drive my desires. I have no choice but to do so, as I already mentioned, I am stuck with myself. The only thing to do is start and keep motivated to see some progress. I remember when I was a teenager, if I didn't see results in 2 weeks, I was done. Experience has taught me that everything to improve yourself takes time. Learning. Building relationships. Losing weight. They all take time and patience.

"Talk to yourself like you would talk to someone you love."

This phrase changed the way I talk to myself entirely when I started practicing it. I thought about the way I talk to my friends and loved ones. Even when the mistake was a stupid one, they were always comforted with understanding. My approach is always to listen to all of the information, ask a few questions, and we talk through some solutions and a course of action based on where we are. There is no berating. I may ask 'why would you do that?' but this is to better understand their frame of mind at the time.

I do the same thing in my own life, but my loved ones don't get the same kind of verbal abuse I used to provide myself with. The fact of the matter is that I am stuck with myself for life, so if I'm not good to myself and treat myself with love, why would I expect somebody else to? I find it very helpful to think of my best friend and what I would say to her instead.

People allow themselves to stay in negative situations because it's easier to stay and suffer. Moving on is definitely not comfortable, similar to moving...it is uncomfortable and sometimes can be scary and takes some time to adjust because it's new. But once you settle in and make yourself comfortable, hindsight will say it wasn't as bad as you thought, after all. Even if it does end up to be that bad, once it's done it won't need to be done again. Once you do it that first time, it gets easier.

Some of the benefits that I can take away from all of the jobs that I did have since I left the one I was at for 10 years is that I learned so much, I was challenged and pushed to learn new things on my own. Learn new things for my positions. Adapt to a changing selling environment. Learn how to communicate better with people. How marketing and sales work in parallel with one another and how to leverage marketing as a sales person. Change can be difficult to manage, but staying somewhere just because it's easy and comfortable is not the life I want to live.

We all have different ideas of what we believe in. It can be God, a 'higher power', I prefer to refer to it as the Universe, since we all know it is out there. If you look at your life and evaluate circumstances and situation that pop up, the Universe is always there guiding you. There is always some invisible magnet moving life in the direction I am intended to go. When I've tried to go against the flow or ignore the message the Universe is trying to send me, I always experience pain. That pain is often what shocks me back into the right direction and magically, all of my situations start to resolve themselves. Trusting the Universe to bring me what I need comes easier because I have seen the times something happened to save me.

To break belief down into simpler terms, I will use affirmations. Many people say things to themselves daily, as a way of motivating and inspiring themselves. I think we all say things to reassure ourselves sometimes. How many people say these things to themselves and actually trust what they are saying to be the truth? I tried posting affirmations around my mirror years ago, as well. Telling myself little things to help me. They encourage me. Like anything in life, speaking words has little impact if there is not action to support it, in this case, the action is to believe the words being spoken.

Chapter 7

Situational Analysis

I don't always see things the same way other people do, which most appreciate, since it offers a different perspective, one they might not have previously considered. I have come to understand, things that are apparent to one person, but not always be as obvious to others. I evaluate situations and relationships based on a number of variables. I will begin with saying that 95% of the time, people will tell you what you want to hear for their own sake less than for yours. While they are telling you what you want to hear, they will be showing you their actual feelings through their behaviors.

There is a man that I have been friends with for close to a decade. We met when we were both single. It seemed as if there was always a mutual attraction. Some of his behaviors, some of our conversations, indicated that the attraction was mutual. But other behaviors did not match up. Like his lack of availability, there was never any available time to hang out or do anything. There was always something else that required his attention. But then one day he met someone and fell in love. Geographically she was a more convenient option. I was upset, but there really isn't anything to be done when someone wants to be with someone else so I moved on. So they got married.

Then when their marriage failed, I heard from him again. I try to keep my feelings at arm's length. But there are people who slip by the gate because we want to see something more. This was someone I thought I had a connection with. I try to maintain my hope in people. So I started seeing and talking to him again. But it was the same as before. Allowing myself to be disappointed, again. I should have learned from my past experience. He always said just enough to keep hope in mind, even if it wasn't true. I'm not embarrassed that I gave something a chance because I had hope it might work out. It's embarrassing because I knew at the back of my mind, from previous experience, that it would not work out. We all have different thresholds for how much we are willing to tolerate. As we gain experience and wisdom, the time it takes to figure out how tolerable a situation is decreases because we have a better bullshit radar.

It has always baffled me that a single man with no children to care for can think that 'I'm so busy' is an acceptable excuse. I've heard this excuse a lot. Offering the benefit of the doubt, I will say this is the line is a deflector. Just something to say, no actual intention behind it. I think it's a way of avoiding someone until they go away. To think anything else would be making excuses because it would be based on imagination and assumption.

One of the things that I ask myself now is: Of all the things that I have done for this person, with an open heart, how many times have they done anything for me? Who keeps this friendship going? It isn't easy to find a genuine person who is willing to support you in your life, if you are that person, realize how valuable it is to have someone you in their corner. If someone can't appreciate your value, no matter who it is, they don't deserve to have it.

I am much more patient than I give myself credit for. I have tried to become more understanding and tolerant. There comes a point when these qualities cross over to the realm of stupidity. There is no need to be tolerant of someone who doesn't consider your time or your feelings. There is no need to be understanding of someone who doesn't reciprocate the friendship you show them. It's ok if 2 people have different values. I accept others for their ideas and respect that everyone has the right to live how they see fit. People don't like being corrected or to be told they are anything other than what they think they are. If someone thinks they are a good person, regardless of the evidence you have to support otherwise, they will stop listening and start defending themselves. So it doesn't make any sense to point out someone's shortcomings, all it does is create animosity. I can only accept that I have the control to choose whether or not I want to continue with the relationship.

I remember saying to my friend once, not everybody deserves your kindness. There are people who appreciate and value having you in their life, you see it and feel the love they have for you in their lives. There are the relationships that you put in more than you get out of them. There came a transition point in my life where I started to realize that **my value is determined by me, not the people I allow into my life**. If I don't acknowledge the benefits I bring to their lives, how can I expect them to see it? I treat others the way

I would like to be treated. So why would I settle for less than what I have to offer?

There are a few reasons why I used to give people a chance before they earned it:

Hope. I believe in love. I have hope that it does exist. I also allow myself to buy in to some of the romantic ideas that sometimes with time and understanding people can change. I think it can bring out the best in people.

Wanting to give people a chance. Hope leads to giving people chances. Most of the time, I have a good idea of how a situation is going to go when I get into it. There are often cues that allow you to see what the other person's goal is. The fact is that regardless of what people say, their behavior will tell you everything you need to know. However, because I am a competitive person by nature, I like to see if I'm right. If I think about it, if I were unable to give people a chance, I probably would not have experienced half the things I have.

Taking people at their word. And wanting to give others a chance leads to trusting what they have to say, at first. Actions will reveal if their words are untrue. The trick is to observe and compare if their actions are consistent with their words.

If you meet a man online and he lives in the same city. He wants to see but can't find time, do his words match up with his actions? What is preventing him from seeing you? This is not the first single man in the world that I have ever met, seems to be a common thing we all seem to forget. Compared to other experiences I have had with single men, this is not regular behavior, there are 2 possible options that I can identify as reasons why.

1.   He is less available than he would like to share.
2.   He isn't THAT interested.

I don't assume that anyone is lying. However, I can determine that despite what he says, he just cannot make time for me, for whatever reason. Is there a reason to be angry? Maybe. But perhaps the better thing to do is just to walk away. Sometimes easier said than done, especially when you have time invested in someone. I consider how many instances of relationships that I have had like this. More than I care to admit. Part of confidence is accepting that you can't control other people. Others are going to do what they want to do based on their wants and needs at the time. If you have a partner, if they want to cheat, they will find a way. No amount of nagging and monitoring is going to change that. It might help you to make it more difficult for them, but they will find a way. The same way if you want to do something badly enough, you will do it, throwing caution to the wind. I try to give people the benefit of the doubt. But until a relationship is a relationship, it's nothing.

Considering relationships I've had with men who treated me well and made time for me. What was the difference between these men, and the ones that were less appreciative of my value? There are many different variables, but I would say the most obvious difference that I observe, is that the men who were indifferent were the ones that didn't have to put forth any effort. I did all the work. They were the ones that I wanted to speak with. The ones that I would make myself available for are exactly the ones that couldn't be bothered with me. So I started doing a bit of research on this subject. This is not rocket science, actually. There are plenty of books and movies about exactly this subject. There is a huge market devoted completely to helping people find love. Think like a Man, Act like a Lady is the perfect example of this. The book was so amazing they made it into a movie. This book is more about using self-evaluation as empowerment to make better decisions without always relying on feedback from others.

I encourage you to evaluate some of your past relationships, or subsequent attempts in that direction.

Was there a man that did not appreciate you?

Maybe he just did the bare minimum to make you happy and to keep you quiet?

How did you end up getting together?

What happened?

Living during a pandemic gave me a lot of time to evaluate my relationships and the value they present me with. When it feels like the world has gone haywire, it's nice to know there is someone there to talk to. Someone who cares about how you are and wants to hear your thoughts and feelings about what is going on in the world. When you can know so many people and have so few that think of you, it gives you something to think about. I can't be angry or resentful. I cultivated the relationships I wanted to be like this. So my biggest lesson in the middle of this pandemic, if you want to keep people at a distance, at a distance they will stay.

I wasn't wrong to keep these people at a distance. I'm not even wrong for having cultivated these relationships in this manner. It worked for me at the time. Life has now presented me with a scenario that has forced me to look at myself more closely and question how happy I am, at this point in my life. And if I have been living my life in consistency with my beliefs today. I'm not, so instead of being angry, or sad, or catering to any negative emotions, I can just start living in terms of my values from this day forward. I don't regret allowing people the opportunity to show me the part of themselves they choose to let me see. It is always up to me, at that point, to decide if I am willing to accept what the other person has to offer.

When I consider how long it has taken me to learn some of things that I have in life, I could be really upset about the time I wasted doing the wrong things. I take consolation, however, in the fact that there are people who live their whole life, and never open their eyes to see the error of their ways. When I think about this part of the population, I'm grateful to have made these realizations when I did. Even if it's later than I would have liked, as the saying goes, better late than never. There is nothing wrong with making mistakes. The fault lies in not learning from them.

Here is a very common example for many women. If I had not realized if a man isn't contacting me, it's because he does not want to. I might continue to put my ego through these situations where I feel rejected by continuing to reach out, allowing myself to be brushed off. There is no need. There are 2 ways you can occupy your mind to not start acting crazy. One way is to find another him to hear from. This can be good and bad. But it is not sustainable. The better way to occupy your mind would be to throw yourself into something that you are passionate about. I love working on my skills, my health, and my mind. If you are going to be obsessed with somebody, be obsessed with the most important person in your life. We all have things we don't like about ourselves, some things we can change, and some things we cannot. Better to focus on the things you can change, figure out what your best assets are, and use them to your advantage, always.

I think every person has come into my life for a reason, some it was for days, others it was for years, very few have and will continue to be there for a lifetime. Feeling regret over experiences we have had a pointless. The least you will get from any relationship you have is the experience of having had it, good or bad. The bare minimum you will learn is how you want or don't want, to be treated. Thinking this ways helps me to not hold any hatred for anybody. Hate is too toxic to keep. Whether it be for your ex who made your life miserable to someone who used you for whatever reason. I think about how exhausting anger and distress is on my body. These feelings don't have enough value to me for me to want to hold on to them.

Many people can't believe in something they can't see, but I believe in Karma with all my heart. Somewhere throughout the course of my life, I noticed a pattern. Every time I did something wrong to someone I would experience the same kind of situation and be on the receiving end, at some point in the future. The punishment was always at least, if not more than 10 times worse than what I did, and it always reminded me of that time I did something bad. There is no set time for when it came back around. Sometimes it took a week, sometimes it took years. But retribution always managed to find me. I accept that if it finds me, it will find anybody who wronged me, as well. This isn't something that requires any effort. All it requires is trust. I won't always know, but I know the ills that I have done to others came right back to me. It gives me the peace of mind that I need to let go of negative feelings and move on from draining emotions. It takes much more energy and is much more exhausting to be angry and negative than it does to be happy and positive.

It's rare that someone who wronged you is going to come and tell you someone did the same thing to them. There have been times that I was informed because of the mutual contacts we might have. But it doesn't matter, regardless. I trust that the Universe will take care of that and move on with my life because to dwell on things is like procrastinating. I don't need to wait for anything to move on.

Chapter 8

"Closure"

A term from my youth that I thought was so necessary for so long. What I came to realize is that closure isn't something most people offer willingly. The truth of the matter is that you don't need anyone but yourself to find closure over relationships that have ended. You can wait the rest of your life for an explanation, but if someone doesn't want to talk about something, they won't. I have also noticed that trying to push the point is not only a waste of time, but also takes focus away from more positive things going on.

I was dating this man one summer for a few months. He said he was single and I believed him. I had no reason not to. We were getting along very well, I liked him a lot. He was doing most of the right things. We had a good time together. I saw him regularly. But I noticed I didn't hear from him in the evenings. This was a red flag, at the back of my mind, but I decided to ignore it. Telling myself, 'let go of your expectations.' Being busy myself and working on my goals, I didn't really think about it too much. I saw him regularly enough, telling myself, 'just let things develop how they will'. His weekends were busy tending to his sick father and his mom, as they were getting on in their years. Understanding at its best…

Then about 3 months later, I just stopped hearing from him. I was upset. I had no warning, no reason, just here today, gone tomorrow. It isn't easy to understand why someone suddenly disappears from your life and becomes unreachable. For a few months, I didn't understand it. I think its human nature to want to know what happened and where you went wrong. Did I say something? It reminded me of past situations where I might have been more insistent on getting some kind of response. It amuses me that I once wanted to give anybody the opportunity to tell me what they think is wrong with me. What I understood, was that the relationship was over, for whatever reason, and there was nothing I could do. The best thing to do was to accept that every outcome is in my best interest and move on.

At the end of the summer, early fall, I found out his girlfriend he was living with gave birth to their child. Horrified is the first word that comes to mind when I think about this time. Then rage. I don't like him, I don't trust him, but I don't hold a grudge against him, either. He reminded me how nice it is to feel secure and comfortable with someone. Sex is not affection and there is nothing that describes love short of magic. I had gone without that for so long I forgot how nice it is to have someone to talk to and spend time with. I choose what I take away from the experiences I have. If I choose to focus on the negatives, I might not want another relationship. By focusing on the positive things I got out of the experience, I gain some insight and confidence for the next one that I have.

Before that point I had convinced myself that superficial relationships were a suitable replacement for a deeper connection because I was too busy to deal with anything more. The truth is when I found something that offered me more, I found the time for it.

A broken heart is the worst feeling in the world. Especially when you have reminders of that person in everything that you do. Not being able to sleep or eat. Not wanting to get out of bed or go to places that I once loved. Having constant reminders of happy times with someone every time you drive by that spot. Even if a romance lasts for a few days, it doesn't diminish the joy that person brought in to your life, even for that short a time. What you felt for each other, in that moment, was real. There is nothing wrong with taking some time to let yourself feel those emotions to heal. The older I get and the more experiences I have, the more I understand.

If there is something to mourn over, appreciate the happiness you experienced and what that person brought in to your life. Every relationship will teach you something about the way you want to be treated and how you want to treat another person. They taught you something about relationships that you did not know before. Every person I have ever known has touched my life in some way because I have learned from each of them. Some continue to teach me. Some were only there for a short time. All lessons have served me at some point in my life, whether I can give them direct credit or not. And if you're mourning over a relationship where you had nothing to appreciate about it, wake up! There's better people in the world who will value you.

It reminds me of a situation I had with my best friend. I told her once, I never saw the relevance to breaking up with one of my girlfriends, and I don't understand why women do that. It's just pointless dramatics to get attention and start an argument. I don't need closure on a relationship with another woman. She thought this was funny and we laughed about it. Then a few months later, I broke up with her.

I was sitting at home one day a few months later, doing nothing special. She came to my mind and I had to ask myself, 'what was the matter with me?' She had 3 small children, was going through a divorce and here I am needing to break up because 'I can't get attention'. I can't even remember what was bothering me anymore. But I remember what she was going through.

When I look back on that time and consider what happened to cause me to do that?

And that's when it dawned on me…I wanted her to modify her ways. All I wanted was for her to reciprocate her interest in our friendship. I was unable to express that into words she could understand so I took a step back. I think my hope was for a grand gesture of apology or for her to come to this great realization that she was wrong. That didn't happen. So we ended up parting ways for a few months, until I started looking beyond myself.

Very similar to our 'break up', and thinking back on the times that I felt 'closure' was so necessary for my heart to be mended, closure was the last effort. It's always the person who was dumped that needs this sense of 'closure'. Why do you suppose that is? Because closure is actually a last effort to get that person back. For them to see what you shared and give them time to reconsider. There is no need to understand why someone doesn't want to be with you anymore. All you really need is to acknowledge that relationship has ended. Looking back on some of my behaviors in an effort to obtain closure, I am happy that I can share my thoughts with others to hopefully save your own egos from suffering the same pains mine has. Once I learned that I don't need to beg anybody to explain why he doesn't want to be with me anymore, the happier I was.

The turning point for me was when I considered how many times had I begged someone to speak with me so I could have my closure? What was I really looking for? Did I really need someone to further articulate to me to reasons he doesn't want to be with me? These are sobering questions because they made me look at myself honestly. It made me really start to wonder…what is this 'closure'? I had seen in on television and in movies, which romanticized rejection, looking back on it. We see movies that almost encourage people to act crazy because we see movies where this one grand gesture is all you need for the other person to 'come to their senses'.

I have learned that it is far more productive and empowering to let people walk out of my life with my dignity intact. Trying to make people stay in your life just causes them to treat you poorly. I have to consider my own actions and beliefs. My dating experiences have also allowed me to appreciate this concept much more because most people have little reason to tell you they aren't interested in seeing you anymore. I think this partly contributes to the 'crazy' girl stereotype. Some people are content to simply ignore you until you 'get the point'. In response to this, depending on a person's age and experience, they might start doing things that seem crazy. Like showing up to 'drop off' items left behind. Finding reasons to keep contact, whether it be some piece of information that might be of mutual interest you want to share or just because you miss them. Allowing yourself to be a story he one day tells his friends about 'the girl who couldn't get over me'. When, in actuality, your actions were driven by emotions and anger rather than an actual desire to recapture anything. It isn't right and it's not fair, but in reality, especially with casual dating and hookups, there is no necessity to end anything.

I was dating this guy for a couple of years that I had worked with previously. When we began seeing each other, he told me he didn't want a relationship. Just to hang out and keep each other company occasionally. I agreed and things were fine for a couple of years. We got along well. We didn't impose ourselves in one another's lives. We saw each other occasionally, but there wasn't any emotional connection. We didn't talk on the phone or keep in regular contact. We got along but things never progressed and there were no hints that any further interest in progressing. So one day, I decided it was over because our values are not the same.

I appreciated the kind of relationship we had in place at the time. I understood that I was in no position to make any demands. If he didn't share the same values that the least you could do for someone you are seeing is to wish them a happy holiday, it isn't my place to ask for it. If someone else's values don't line up with mine, it's not my place to tell anybody what they should do. If it was something he wanted to do, he would. Not providing this basic respect, is also giving me some indication as to the bigger picture, as well. Do I want to be that girl who's just 'hanging around' until someone better comes along?

That leads to the question, how do you end a relationship that isn't a relationship? My logical mind told me you don't. It isn't a relationship. I believe in letting people be who they are. I just stopped talking to him. Stopped texting and answering text messages. I think I heard from him once 6 months later and then I didn't hear from that guy again. He didn't put much effort into the relationship, so why would he put much into keeping it together? If neither have anything invested in a relationship, there is no need to 'wrap things up' when things end.

If someone doesn't have to put any effort in to getting to know you, it's because they don't want to. Most of the instances that I can think of where I didn't put any effort into getting to know somebody were easier to disappear on. It works both ways. I struggle with the idea of opening up to people. I think most single people know it's easier to date without getting attached if you don't get to know the other people too deeply. You also feel less rejected if someone doesn't know you more intimately on an emotional level. I think about the times that I did open up and let someone get to know me. These were the times that I felt the loss of their presence and was more compelled to want to know what happened to change the situation.

Chapter 9

Shedding Expectations

I don't compare people to one another. If a man I was seeing was that great and it was such a wonderful relationship, I would still be with him. This actually makes him not a good person to measure anybody against. Many people compare their current relationship to the last one, regardless of how they were treated. But if you're trying to break the patterns of your failed relationships, why would you compare your current success to a past failure? I've noticed in myself and others that this can create expectations of the other person. You expect them to behave or respond to you in a particular way and start creating situations for them to fall into someone else's behaviors because it's what you're used to.

If you must compare, use someone who makes you feel good about yourself. Someone from a past relationship, because most relationships start off wonderful until the end, is a reminder that if you felt it that time, you can feel it again. Every interaction is different and teaches you something about what you want or don't want. If you have no one you can think of, that's ok. That's where it comes in handy not to compare anybody. Everybody has been through their own traumas and sees the world from their own lenses.

I see each person for who they are. This does not mean that I forget all of the experiences I have had. Quite the opposite. While you can't assume that one person is like another, there are certain behaviors that are common among all. For instance, when someone feels accused, they get defensive. When people are lying, most people start getting shifty eyes. Not always, but these are general commonalities. The real intention, however, is to use your past experience to ask intelligent questions to help get to the root of the situation without accusing or making anyone feel attacked.

It isn't easy and it is extremely sobering to be able to look at myself objectively and to accept my flaws. I understand why people don't do it. It can be very painful to realize truths and shatter beliefs about yourself. I have cried a number of times having realizations about myself that I was embarrassed to know. The good thing is that once I realize something, I can't unlearn that realization. All I can do from that point on, is change myself to reflect how I want to present myself to the world.

The truth is that few people want to take ownership of situations to themselves, never mind admit it to another person. I observed one of my close friends' marriage over the years. It evolved from being very connected and together to somewhat fragmented over the years. Buying a home, working on your careers, having and raising children, dealing with finances, the list of things that can dampen the romance can go on forever. But their relationship stayed together. Over the years she mentioned his complaints. She slept too much. She doesn't show him any attention. He wanted her time and was arguing with her about it. She was just too tired. It's hard to be a mother with a demanding full time job. The one day, she finds out he's having an affair.

Obviously, and justifiably, she is shocked, hurt and enraged. And these are all understandable reactions. So during the process of trying to see if they can move past this obstacle in their relationship, she takes zero ownership because she didn't do anything wrong. This makes complete sense to me. She does not believe any of her actions contributed to the end result because she personally did nothing wrong.

I don't believe any circumstance I find myself in can be blamed entirely on another person. I understand why she might not want to take ownership of her contributions to this situation going the direction that it did. I'm not saying he's right, I'm not saying don't be mad at him. What I am saying is that it's important to understand that 2 people arrived at that point in their life together. So 2 people should own their part of the events leading up to that affair.

This isn't self-criticism. It's learning from experience. I don't need to share these self-discoveries with anybody, which is what makes it possible for me to look at myself honestly. I can lie to everybody in the world, but at the end of the day, what sense does it make for me to lie to myself? It's about seeing where improvements can be made. If I can do this regularly towards being a better employee and improving my profession, why wouldn't I apply the same assessment to my life? Where I can work towards being a better person.

Look at experiences with someone from an "outside looking in" perspective. How did their behaviors change compared to what I am accustomed to? What, if anything, am I doing differently? Is there some reason for their change in attitude? Experience is not wasted, there is always a lesson to be learned in every situation. If I don't look at myself from an objective perspective and own my mistakes, how am I supposed to identify my 'weaknesses'? This is not an exercise to compare my flaws to anybody or seek a different opinion because only I know my behavior and what I'm thinking. Before I reached this level of observation and awareness, I made the same mistake over and over. Just because you don't want to have the same experience again doesn't mean you won't if you don't do something differently.

My greatest epiphany when I started writing this book is that I cannot expect someone else to value me until I acknowledge and accept my own value. It is very easy to allow your mind to sway you in the direction you are biased towards. Growing up, I thought I wanted one single monogamous marriage, some kids, etc. even as a single parent, to some degree.

If you meet enough people who just want to 'hook up and have a good time', you start to believe that this is what single people today are looking for. This is not the case. Most people want to be loved. Most people want a relationship, but they prefer to go with the 'Friends with Benefits' model out of convenience.

When someone says they don't want a relationship, there are a few reasons:

1. They are just getting out of a relationship and need some time to heal/find themselves/play the field/ have new experiences

2. They don't want a relationship with you. You are suitable to 'mate' with, but do not qualify as a partner.
3. They don't want to get hurt. So they will maintain emotional distance from everyone.

The truth of the matter is if someone fitting their idea of the ideal partner comes along, they would be ready. It is a perceived kindness to tell someone 'I'm not looking for a relationship, but we can still hang out'.

If this isn't what you want, to put your own value aside, for the sake of 'hanging out' because someone isn't looking for something serious undermines your own value and what you have to offer. The best way I can illustrate this point is diamonds. We assign high value to them, they are precious and rare but not everybody can afford them. They are not a common commodity for most people. If everyone could have one, they would like a cubic zirconia. Cubic zirconia are much more common and affordable. Anyone can get one. Would I rather be a diamond or a cubic zirconia? Diamond buyers are just as rare. Diamonds are precious. You don't come across them as often. This makes the cubic zirconia a more obvious assumption. With time, you start to realize the diamond buyers are equally worth the wait. But if you know you're a diamond but want to look like a cubic zirconia, you're going to get low-balled every time.

I cannot keep creating the same situation because I assume who someone is and how they are going to treat me based on my previous experience. Meeting someone who you think is wonderful because he treats you in a way that makes you happy is a wonderful thing. Having faith is trusting that every experience is different in its own way and that by expecting someone to behave a certain way, they will, because you are creating that in the Universe.

Faith is something many people think they have. Many people say mantras daily. But do they trust that what they are saying is their truth? I believe there is a 'Higher Power' that I call the Universe instead of God. It is a physical entity everyone can relate to. Faith is not just believing or reciting mantras and prayers. Trusting that those words are being heard and will deliver you what you need is what matters. It won't show up by FedEx, so you need to keep yourself open to possibilities that cross your path.

The Universe is always sending us the things we desire, all we need to do it be open to receiving. Sometimes it doesn't come in the shape and form we expect, which is often why we won't see it. When my life is particularly painful, or I start experiencing things that don't feel right, I revisit my goals and see how far I have strayed from the course I know I am supposed to be on. Once I get back on the right road, things usually have a way of working themselves out again. The Universe guides and helps navigate our way through life if we choose to see the signs. I love shows and movies from the renaissance era. Game of Thrones. Vikings. The Last Kingdom. One of the things that I admire about these depictions is the level of faith people possessed in this time period. I am not speaking about the religions themselves, but the deep trust the people had in their version of God. Their faith may have been extreme, in this day and age, but is nonetheless admirable.

Over time, this has obviously changed, with the advancement of science, new hopes arise. Belief in faith now intersects with medicine and technology. People still hold on to their faith, but can still opt to do everything they can to treat and care for the people they love to help their prayers along. At the end of the day, none of us controls when we leave this world. All we can do is the best we can and have faith that, no matter the situation, every outcome is in my best interest.

I look back on my dating experiences with a critical eye and wonder at the levels of understanding I have achieved now compared to when I first started. Whether someone does or doesn't do something, they are still sending a message. If someone doesn't call, or cancels plans, for instance, I was more inclined to make an excuse under the veil of being understanding. Things happen, absolutely. Maybe show up late because they are disorganized. But to make plans with someone and then magically not hear from him the day of the event, rarely does this happen. I allowed others to undervalue my time and attention because I didn't recognize the value in myself.

When I consider myself and the way I move through life, I make time for the things that matter to me. This is not a foreign concept to anybody. Everyone I allow into my space is taking up my most precious commodity of time. If they can't value that and me, I understand, but I don't have to accept it. People treat you the way you allow them treat you. If someone always cancels on you and ignores your messages, even if their intentions aren't negative, they're just thoughtless, this is still telling you something.

Listening to stories from my friends, I started to wonder, what makes these people so important. I used to have a great need to understand why people behave the way they do.

We all have our own sets of values and characteristics who make us who we are. I think about myself, the people who mean the most to me are positive they can count on me. I keep my word and if I say something, I am going to do it. I think this can be said for most people. You show up in life, for the people that matter most. There have been too many occasions that I can remember where my empathy was a vehicle for me to allow someone to treat me poorly.

It comes down to priorities. If someone is important to you, you make time for them. Same rule applies when you meet someone interesting. I see it every day where we come up with excuses for someone who never offered one in an effort to prove we are empathetic to their position in life. 'I'm busy' has somehow become the default response when you don't hear from somebody. And in an effort to not be that 'crazy woman', we accept being treated less than we treat others. I think of how many times I trusted that someone was going to do what they said they would, only to find out that their words were meaningless.

By observing the most significant friendships I have in place, I have to recognize that I am not lacking anything in my life. I think about all of the things I have been through in my life, without support and comfort, and remind myself that this isn't a need, this is a want. It might be nice to have, but it has never been necessary. I have the love and support that I need to get me through. When I think about all of the relationships I've had, the longest and most significant ones have always been with people who pushed me to rely on myself. There have been times that I was envious of my friends who had someone to share their lives with. I'm happy to appreciate that my life is full and if I am meant to fall in love, one day, I will.

I worked with a woman once, who was not the most social personality. She was lovely, just more of an introvert. She met her husband at work and got married. They also got divorced one child and a few years later. Her position in the company, her personality type, and being a single mother all contributed to her not socializing much. For years we worked together and I knew she was lonely. She wanted to meet someone to share her life with, to help raise her daughter with. She was also friends with a man we worked with for a number of years, as well. They got to know each other. He made time for her regularly to see how she was doing, how her day was going. That blossomed into a relationship down the road, when he told her how he was feeling and they got married. You never know when and where love might find you.

I remember being unhappy about being alone and realizing one day 'It isn't that nobody wants to be with you. You don't want to be with the people available right now. So there is no reason to feel sad. If you were that sad, you would be with someone'. When looking at it this way, it's hard to stay in that place of sadness. Whether or not you know it, there is somebody, somewhere, who wants to be with you. Whether you want them or not, they still desire you.

I used to be friends with a woman who has been single for her whole life. She has never experienced living with a man. She had relationships, but nothing ever blossomed in to anything serious. This was something that really bothered her. I can see where the frustration in that might be. She is an extremely confident and successful woman. She lives a healthy lifestyle. Goes on vacations with her friends when she pleases. If she loses her job, she doesn't have to worry about money because she has a nest egg to rely on. I know couples who aren't able to establish that kind of security and fun in their lives together.

She had a vision of the kind of relationship she wanted. I've studied the laws of attraction and understand you need to be very clear on the qualities you want a partner to have, she had that figured out. What I have realized is the Universe doesn't interpret desires in a negative or positive or a masculine and feminine way. All it knows is what you think of is what it will send. It doesn't determine if that will come in the shape of a partner or a friend. Friends are also a source of companionship and support. Every quality she was looking for in a partner was already present in her life. She had many friends she could depend on for love, support, comfort and any other need she might have in a relationship. The only thing lacking was a physically intimate partner.

One of the things I have learned is that it takes a brave person to say how they feel, regardless of what they are going to hear from the other person. Every failed experience brings you that much closer to the 'one'.

I also accept that people are going to treat me how they're going to treat me, the question is if I allow them to do so. My time isn't valuable because I gave someone the impression that my time didn't matter. What they think is irrelevant, because I choose to accept this behavior by doing and saying nothing about it. This is not a spring board to talk about standing up for yourself and telling people off, although, I think I have done that in the past, as well. I have come to a point where if someone is unable to reinforce their statements with corresponding actions, it isn't my job to say anything. My only responsibility is to decide whether or not this situation is worth my time anymore.

I used to be bothered by other people's lack of consideration. It is frustrating to make time for someone else and not hear from them or have your plans cancelled at the last minute. Nobody wants to make a big deal about it, things happen. Things do happen, I understand this. For the majority of my single life, I thought this was the right thing to do. My never ever is to never ever look psycho. I allowed myself to get the impression that standing up for myself might make me appear crazy or unstable. So I accepted less than I deserve because, at the end of the day, I wanted someone to like me more than I wanted to love myself.

Conversations are worth having. I hold more value in behavior and actions, but I think that some conversations matter. If I say something, it is being said because I mean it. If someone were to say, for example, that they want to lose weight, but don't do anything to modify their behaviors or change their diet, how seriously are they about losing weight? The same principal applies to conversations.

I reinforce my words by performing the corresponding actions to substantiate them. I've learned not to let these things upset me as much as they used to looking at them from a black and white perspective. If someone is interested, they don't hide it. If they are telling you they're interested, but their behavior says something else, they are telling you something. Despite what their personal issues are. We all have personal issues, but somehow, manage to make time for the things and the people we care about.

Chapter 10

Fear of failure

Fear of failure can be paralyzing. It stops a lot of people from trying. Nobody wants to be ridiculed for committing their thoughts to paper, for example. One of the fears I've carried from youth is birthday parties. When my son was growing up, I always made sure he attended parties he was invited to because my deepest fear has always been to have a party nobody showed up to. I got over that fear to have parties for him, because it was his desire and because, when I thought about it, it seemed a ridiculous fear to have.

Fear of failure and fear of success are both come down to not believing you are deserving of success. Both come from an internal place. In the last few years I have become inquisitive about successful people. What is their secret? There are so many examples in the world of people who overcame amazing obstacles to become the people they are today. People who used their medical issues and personal challenges to launch them to new heights in their lives. Used their lives as an example to help others live better lives. I started watching YouTube videos and listening to podcasts. There are so many amazing people to inspire, so many amazing stories to be told.

I have learned to use my fear of failure to drive me, instead of paralyze me. I reframed my thinking around this subject. Not trying is the beginning of failure. Instead of being afraid of failing, I'm afraid of what happens if I don't try. When your desire to do something outweighs your fears, this is often when people act. I don't want to wait till I'm under pressure to be great. I've often considered some of the things that I have accomplished and the experiences that I've had and wonder what can I do if I apply this pressure to myself? Then I look at professional athletes and Olympians and say, "That is what you can accomplish". Some people are pushed by someone they love like a parent or a spouse. Others are pushed by the circumstances of their life and feel they have no choice. And then there is that small sliver of the population that has it embedded in their DNA that they must achieve their goals. In all of these cases, however, it's a compelling reason to push forward. Even when you are scared.

Fear of success is a bit more difficult. It's almost silly to say that you're afraid of the light at the end of the dark tunnel. I understand it. I prefer anonymity. Large crowds and too many people all at once can be overwhelming for me. Getting everything you want seems like a scary thought. I don't even think I realized it until I started to really think about it. A common example is when someone gets into a relationship and things are going great. One day one partner decides to start wondering, 'Is it for real? They can't be for real, there's got to be something wrong with them.' The mind starts racing, doubt begins and eventually things start happening for obstacles to come up.

I wonder how many people experience both fear of failure and fear of success. Fear of failure is what will stop you from starting and then along the way might jump out of a dark corner here and there. Fear of success, for me, is more a fear of the unknown. No matter the amount of positive thinking, if something is not meant to be, it will not be. That has never been a bad thing, everything always works out in my favor. I wasn't able to let go of things until I came to this understanding.

If I don't get what I wanted in life, that was for a good reason.

Using a very simple example, I can best relate it to a movie. Sometimes I'll see commercials for movies that look so amazing. Excitedly waiting for months, in anticipation of the release date. Then the day comes that I finally get to go see this movie that I thought was going to be so great and it wasn't. There might have been something I came across on Netflix a couple of weeks before that I loved. Sometimes you don't have to buy in to the hype.

I don't always know the reason, but this thought gives me immense comfort. I don't know how to lightly coax myself into getting over fear. It doesn't make sense to my logical mind. So I have to push myself past it. I don't have time to understand the root cause of some of my issues. Truthfully, some I would rather not relive. I ask myself every day, what can I do right now, today? The past is in the past, all I can do is accept it and keep going. We all come from different places, environments, backgrounds, beliefs. There are things that have happened in my life that have left scars. But I don't believe in using them as an excuse to stop me from moving forward. I refuse to allow myself to stop because I'm afraid of what I can accomplish, that's irrational. We all have growth and contributions to make to the world. My responsibility is to do my part and show up. Do my best and not let myself get blocked by the figments of my imagination.

Another component is feeling like a fraud. Like you'll 'be found out' one day. It comes down to feeling undeserving. Donald Trump is actually an exceptional example. Many people all around the world have so many opinions about this man I share my birthday with. (That's what prompted my interest in him, to begin with.) Whatever people have to say about this man, he is nothing short of incredible. He has proven himself to be not the most brilliant man in the world, but has rebuilt wealth multiple times. He was famous before he was President. How much criticism did he receive? How many times has he been roasted and ridiculed? Then he ran for office and was voted President of the United States. Obviously, I don't know him, but I'm sure there was some sliver of doubt, some fraction of fear that he might have lost. But I think his desire to be President, his belief in himself, outweighed any fear he might have had to run at all. I may not agree with many of his thoughts and beliefs, but I admire how he has built his life because of the resolve he had to reach his goals.

Ambition is not an innate quality. This is something that is learned. Olympians and other professional athletes, for example. How many of them started out not being very good at their sport? All of them dedicate a majority of their early lifetime to perfecting their crafts and being the best they can be. Whether they are being pushing and motivated by their parents and families or not, at some point, they take ownership of their ambitions. They don't think about failing. Their focus is on success. Improving, getting better.

I think about the times that I tried something new and failed. Sometimes the biggest embarrassment that I had was admitting failure to myself. It made me want to start learning about people following their dreams. Finding out how they became someone worth knowing about. Who was Arnold Schwarzenegger before he found the passion to be Mr. Universe? How did Tony Robbins go from nothing to where he is today? What were their stories? How did they use their experience to drive them forward in life? We often look at successful people and admire and them once they have earned their way into the spotlight. We all have admiration for some famous rapper or actor/actress who suffered for years doing menial jobs most of us don't know about. The person who was focused on perfecting their talents and doing whatever they had to do to survive, until they go their big break is less glamorous than who they are today. I never really thought to find out about what their lives were like before success happened before. They become much more relatable when you start looking at the stories behind the people.

Dedication and drive are not things we are born with. They are things that are born from passion and desire to give something back to the world. Some people reach success with little talent because their dedication and drive compensate for their lack of ability. I admire the people who never took no as an answer. The people who believe in themselves, in spite of people not believing in them. The people who refuse to accept failure as their final outcome. I don't just admire these people, I want to be one of them. A life that is not lived to the fullest is not worth living. My idea of a life lived is not always going to be the same as someone else's.

Experience shapes someone's perception of the world, where one person has experienced assistance and support throughout their life, someone who had to do things on their own will approach the world differently. This applies to anything in life. My best friend and I could not be more different, when it comes to travel. For her, vacations are essential, they need to happen regularly and it needs to be leaving home for a destination. In my opinion, I don't deserve it right now, vacations distract from my goals. I see the truth in what she says, but for the better part of my life, I couldn't go on vacation, there was no time. I have too many things I need to accomplish. I have my priorities. I can do that later, in the meantime I can have enjoy life on weekends and holidays. My rational mind knows that taking breaks is rejuvenating. But I always have this little voice in my head telling me, 'you have to reach your goals first, you can take a vacation when you get where you need to be.'

Expectations is something that we will abandon because we are afraid of the reality and don't want to be disappointed. It became wrong, to expect consideration and respect when I expect a lot from myself. It's a bitter pill to swallow to know that I allowed me to fool myself for so long. The truth is I compromised my expectations in the past for companionship. I have no reason to beat myself up. Navigating dating isn't easy and even if you do have a strong character, sometimes you want to shed your regular self to experience something new. Sometimes, there are instances where I do things with an idea of what the outcome will be. Maybe it's because I hope I'm wrong and want a different outcome. Maybe it's because I don't care. I want what I want because I want it. Sometimes it's one or the other, and other times it's both.

This doesn't mean start imposing expectations on others. Quite the opposite. The expectations now fall on me to identify people who share the same values and stop accepting less than I deserve from the people I choose to have in my life. I need to expect more from myself in selecting the right people to spend my most precious commodity with…my time. Considering all of the information that I have been gathering. The many stories I heard through sharing stories and experiences with my friends because we could identify with one another. Instead of focusing on the negative and the things that could potentially make me feel shame and guilt, I look at how that time enriched my life, and the lives of those around me. What are the lessons that I've learned? More importantly, is to start applying these lessons immediately. Knowledge is wasted if you don't use it. Waiting till tomorrow to do something you can do today is wasting a day of your life.

It's hard to open yourself up to someone, to show them who you are, share your thoughts and feelings. All to be refused or rejected or even worse, taken advantage of. Putting up barriers and walls is something we all do as a self-preservation mechanism. It's easier to let someone leave your life if you didn't have too much invested in them, either. Getting used to talking to someone, sharing a window into your life. To have them all of a sudden gone, one day. I understand how someone could go crazy. I think about some of the pains my heart has suffered in the past and have certainly built some walls myself, over the years. The first thing I can revel in is that I lived through it. Time really does heal all wounds. I think back on some of the most profound pains in this moment and feel nothing but relief to have moved past those times.

Doing nothing is worse than failing. I have to ask myself, would I prefer to wonder 'what if?' I think a lot of the experiences I've had in my life were had because I don't like wondering. If it is something that I want enough now to know I'll wonder about it later, I'll do it now. There may have been tons of flaws in my execution, but I still learned something. I think awareness has always come to me when it would serve me best. Thinking about some of the mistakes I've made, thinking about all of the years I was doing the wrong things, I can understand wanting to give up. I can't be unhappy about the way I was living before I became aware of certain things. The failure to move into the future taking these lessons into consideration is where I would be doing myself a disservice.

Final chapter

The Evolution of me

We all make a conscious decision of who we want to be. The thought of being a failure is paralyzing. The first time I lost a job, I was panicked. Anyone who has been fired knows it's a horrible feeling. The initial shock of being laid off when you know you are in debt and have another person depending on you is terrifying. The first couple of times this happened, my first reaction was fear, panic and despair. Then one time it happened, perhaps it was because it had happened before, I was actually relieved to not have to work at that miserable place anymore. There was no feeling of panic and dread. It's never a good feeling to know I didn't succeed, but there is also recognizing that if I'm not happy about my situation, I can do something to change it. My job is to believe there is something better on the horizon and keep moving forward. Even if you don't see the destination, focus on the horizon, you will still be moving in the right direction.

When I go through tough times, I've learned to look for the opportunity because hard times will always manage to find me. When I think about all of the different kinds of people that have passed through my life, I can say there are 3 kinds of people. Those who give up once hard times come knocking. There are the people who do what they must to live their life. This is the majority of the population. Then there are those people who somehow manage to see through the fog. They don't let anything stop them. Their failures drives their passions and help them get better. They create their own opportunities. They see beyond the here and now and look at the bigger picture. They keep pushing forward because they don't see any other option.

I used to think I needed a perfect situation to have a great life. I used to think about a great retirement and what I would do when I don't have to work anymore. Then it occurred to me one day….why am I going to waste today waiting until tomorrow to enjoy my life? I still stop myself from doing things, my excuse is needing the right circumstances to go on vacation. I have to reframe that idea because life rarely offers the perfect situation to follow a dream. Waiting doesn't do anything but cheat me out of meaningful experiences. I've been putting it off for 3 years and counting. That's one of my personal barriers, but this applies to many situations in life. We impose stipulations on ourselves, waiting for the perfect moment instead of focusing on now. Today.

Many people let life pass by them in anticipation of the future. Do what you can with what you have available to you. This is what I consciously think about as I move through the world. If you don't have money, invest time into finding alternative sources, free information is plentiful in this day and age. If you want to educate yourself in something and can't afford it, we live in a time where information is endless.

Access to anything is possible. This life is the only one I have, it's up to me to decide what I want to do with it and how I want it to be lived. I choose how people think of me and remember me.

Emotions have always been inconvenient for me. I feel too much. I understand them, I feel them very deeply, but I don't like using them. Ever since I was young, being an older child, I was always in a place of making decisions. Most of the time, I would need to keep myself composed and together in situations of crisis because my siblings were at least 4 years younger than I was. There was no room for everybody to get hysterical. In my adult life, with my friends and family, it's similar. I don't know how I manage to keep a calm manner. When I do find myself losing my composure, I take a step back from the situation. Most of the time, there are few situations that have come up that I needed to respond immediately.

There is no shame in taking some time to make a decision. Crying and feelings are necessary. Even if I do it in the privacy of my bed, I still let them come out. They will come out anyways, better to let them flow through you instead of letting things collect, eventually causing an outburst.

I once used to try to ignore or think about something else to avoid, I figured out once you let it flow through you, it goes away. You can only cry so much before you run out of tears. Once the tears are gone, the pain dulls and I'm able to move the situation to the past. If something doesn't work out, in spite of the feelings that I may experience, I choose to believe it's in my best interest. Spending time wallowing in misery isn't as productive as offering your time and attention to someone else who needs it more. It's a mutually beneficial resolution. Even in sorrow, there can be joy, if we let it find us.

I used to be resistant to advice. There was a point when I might have listened, but I didn't hear what people were saying. After your kids are first born is a great example. Everybody has advice on how to raise a child. Everybody knows what they're doing. It can get you in a mindset to just stop listening to what other people have to say. But sometimes, with babies, after you've tried everything and still get no results, you become more open to suggestions. The things that I have been through are experiences I needed to have because I chose to have them. I do not intend to go through them again, but I also want to share those experiences to help others, to help their lives be better.

Most people have good intentions. Most people want to help. I've learned to manage the conversations that I have with people better. I listen to the advice they have to offer because I want to be heard when I speak. If I choose to take their input or not is irrelevant. The point is to give that person the opportunity to be heard and to evaluate if this is advice I want to use. If I don't want help, I won't talk about my problems. If I'm talking to someone who complains, I let them talk about their issues and come up with solutions, or steer their thinking in a more uplifting direction. A relationship can work one of 2 ways with a negative and a positive person. Either the positive person will bring the negative person up. Or the positive person will be brought down by the negative person.

The chemistry of each relationship is different. People relate to one another in different ways. What I might say in this book, might resonate with one person but make another person angry. Where one person might see hope, another sees despair. If someone is too weighted down in misery and won't let me help lift them, I must walk away for my own sake. It doesn't make anybody a bad person to do what is in their best interest. I want to help everybody, but I have come to see there are some cases that I am not the person to help, for whatever reason.

A full seat cannot be occupied. Part of the consolation when relationships end is that it makes space for something else. I can relate to wanting to fill that space when the seat stays empty for long enough. I have approached my life the way I wanted, willing to accept the mistakes I have made along the way. I have no one to blame for the circumstances of my life but myself. Things happen to everybody, what matters is the way I respond and react when things happen to me. We all choose our own path and consciously or not, decide who we want to be. Mistakes and failures are a gift to be learned from to help us evolve. It takes time to figure out. The different paths in life we all take are what equip us with the skills we need to move forward or help someone else in the future.

212 degrees is the point at which water boils, creating steam. That's all it takes is one degree to transform water from liquid to gas. When this concept was presented to me, it made me start thinking about my own life. When things hadn't worked, up to that point, I always wanted to make drastic changes to change my lives. Drastic changes aren't always possible and truthfully, when you have responsibilities, they can be inconceivable. But after I saw the 212 rule, I started approaching life differently. Instead

of thinking about making major changes, why not start looking at the small things in my life that I can change? A whole new world opens up when you start appreciating and improving the life you have instead of waiting for something better to happen.

The things I talk about in this book work the same. For the most part, often, there are only small degrees of change that need to take place to see a difference in life. Nothing happens overnight. Especially when it comes to the way we think about ourselves. I have mental perceptions that I can't help having but small degrees of change in my thinking, small actions can go a long way towards becoming the person you want to be. Nothing amazing was ever built in a day, it became a reality one day at a time. Instead of feeling a need to change myself entirely, now I look at things about myself I would like to change. What I can change, I will apply the 1 degree of change principal. Often, it only takes slight changes to realize success. Staying on course and not getting frustrated enough to give up are the main dangers.

There are always reasons to stop me from doing things in life I want to do. But when thinking back on the things that I accomplished that I didn't conceive as possible, I amaze myself. Nothing was driving me but the need to get my life back on track. What could I do if I instilled that urgency in myself, before I find myself in these kinds of situations again? My goal is to see what I can accomplish by driving myself, before misfortune finds me. Looking for the good in every situation has always helped me find consolation when challenges present me the opportunity to rise above them.

I am learning to accept that I'm human. There are often times that I find myself in a place where I want to give up. That lasts for about a minute and then I force myself to do what I have to do. The majority of the battle is getting there. Many of the things I tell myself have been mentioned in this book. That I only have so much time and I need to use what I have wisely. There is no need to wait to do anything, the hardest part is starting…as long as I have my passion to drive me, it isn't work. Opening up my mind and sharing how I think and process information is a terrifying idea to me, but I have nothing to lose and everything to gain. I have faith in myself.

When I was young, I wanted to be an artist. My parents, being of traditional values and thinking, didn't think that I would be able to make a sufficient living as an Artist. I understand they gave me the best advice they could and had my best intentions at heart. Now, I see that I should probably have followed my talents and not abandoned them along the way. I could say it's my parents fault I gave up my Art to pursue other, more lucrative ventures. I went to school with a girl who took art classes with me for years. I think back and still marvel at how talented she was when we were teenagers. The truth, now that I look back, I didn't trust in my own talent. I compared myself to that girl I went to school with, and told myself I wasn't good enough. I look at the world we have cultivated, where so many people have created their own companies, positions, products. Many coming from humble means, with nothing more than their dream and a desire to make it real.

This is the first major lessons the Universe offered me, about following my dreams. Because Art was my passion in youth. I still love it. Creating or spectating. The beauty in the world is overwhelming. It took decades for me to realize this lesson. I remind myself of this now, when I consider giving up on something that I want. If I consider listening to others and valuing their opinion over my own. Merely to compare myself to someone else, is doing myself a disservice. With the benefit of experience and wisdom, now know that we each have different kinds of Art to offer the world. That doesn't make one better or worse than the other. Just different to accommodate the many flavors of the world.

Our lives are the same, with each of us offering different talents and skills. I don't know what it's like to live in someone else's life, I know what it is to live in mine. I can't judge someone else when I don't know where they're coming from and what their experiences are with the world. All I can do is to first and always, love myself first, because if I don't, I can't expect anybody else to. And second, try to be empathetic to their situation, if possible. We all have doubts and fears…and regrets. The point of life, is to push yourself past those feelings so you can avoid having to feel regret for missed opportunities.

There are so many mistakes I've made that have helped me improve myself, when I got over my ego's pain and use those feelings for something productive. Sometimes it's easier to hold on to the pain and use it as an excuse to cheat yourself out of experiences. There is nothing wrong with needing to hit pause. To be looking for a way to become the person you want to be, for yourself and the people you love. I wanted to share something with the people, particularly the women, who would rather do something productive with that pain, if they must focus on it. To use it to inspire you to greater heights and achieve the things you did not think you could. Even in failure, there is success because most people stop themselves before they even try.

I hope I accomplished my mission.

About the Author

Sharon was born and raised in Montreal. She got into a long term relationship at 21, and became single in her early thirties. She has a passion for people and communication, and leveraged a career in sales to exploit that interest.

As a single mother, she had to figure out how to date and have a social life, while raising her son alone, within the parameters of her own values and principals. Having had a long term relationship in her youth allowed her the opportunity to embrace being single in a unique way and not feel rushed to get into another one lightly. But she still spent a considerable amount of time stumbling around in the dark and making mistakes, trying to figure things out.

She learned to believe that every experience and relationship is presented for a purpose, there is always a lesson to be learned. Instead of letting circumstances defeat her, she uses them as opportunities to challenge her abilities.

But it all started with learning to be honest with herself and seeing where she could improve.

Her perspective on life and relationships is unique and honest. Helping women empower each other and improve their lives is her passion and what drove her to start sharing her experiences. She sees herself in an honest way and owns her accountability in every situation. Her approach and perspective has always been welcome by those who sought to learn it. Her inspiration for writing comes from her friends and the advice she has offered over the years through her experiences.

Her goal is to share her thoughts with as many women as possible, and to help each of them feel empowered and confident.

Printed in the United States
By Bookmasters